"Jordan Seng has shared the principles fr[...]
With A Mission training schools all over the Pacific and has effectively equipped many of our workers to step out and pray for the sick and move in supernatural power. He doesn't write from a theological ivory tower. His teaching is backed up with practical stories and experiences from the trenches. I know that Jordan and the church he pastors are truly missional, practicing the principles laid out in *Miracle Work* on the streets and in the neighborhoods where real people live and hurt. *Miracle Work* will equip you to do the same!"

DANNY LEHMANN, director of the College of Christian Ministries, Youth With A Mission, and author of *Before You Hit the Wall*

"When people are suffering, they don't need normal. They need something different. Fortunately, God provides it through you. The great coaching in this book will explain how you can get involved in miracle work and bring God's love to the world."

MARK DAHLE, author of *How to Pray For Healing (and what to do if nothing happens)*

"Jordan Seng's book is extraordinarily helpful because it answers the 'How?' and 'So what?' questions being asked by real people. I've seen nothing else like it. It's for everyone looking for sane, intelligent, practical instruction about the miraculous power of God in the twenty-first century."

CALEB MASKELL, Society of Vineyard Scholars

"Instantly engaging. *Miracle Work* is down to earth and practical, and full of great stories. Jordan's book has inspired me to seek more of the Holy Spirit's power in our youth ministry and given some very easy ways to apply these concepts."

CHRIS HERNING, senior high pastor, Vineyard Christian Church, Evanston, Illinois

MIRACLE
WORK

A DOWN-TO-EARTH GUIDE
TO SUPERNATURAL MINISTRIES

JORDAN SENG

IVP Books

An imprint of InterVarsity Press
Downers Grove, Illinois

InterVarsity Press
P.O. Box 1400, Downers Grove, IL 60515-1426
World Wide Web: www.ivpress.com
E-mail: email@ivpress.com

Second edition ©2013 by Jordan Seng
First edition ©2012 by Jordan Seng

InterVarsity Press® is the book-publishing division of InterVarsity Christian Fellowship/USA®, a movement of students and faculty active on campus at hundreds of universities, colleges and schools of nursing in the United States of America, and a member movement of the International Fellowship of Evangelical Students. For information about local and regional activities, write Public Relations Dept., InterVarsity Christian Fellowship/USA, 6400 Schroeder Rd., P.O. Box 7895, Madison, WI 53707-7895, or visit the IVCF website at <www.intervarsity.org>.

All Scripture quotations, unless otherwise indicated, are taken from the Holy Bible, Today's New International Version®, NIV® Copyright © 1973, 1978, 1984, 2010 by Biblica, Inc.™ Used by permission. All rights reserved worldwide.

While all stories in this book are true, some names and identifying information in this book have been changed to protect the privacy of the individuals involved.

Design: Cindy Kiple
Interior design: Beth Hagenberg
Images: Philip J. Brittan/Getty Image

ISBN 978-0-8308-3764-9

Printed in the United States of America ∞

Library of Congress Cataloging-in-Publication Data

Seng, Jordan, 1967-
  Miracle work / Jordan Seng.
       pages cm
  Includes bibliographical references.
  ISBN 978-0-8308-3764-9 (pbk. : alk. paper)
 1. Church work. 2. Healing--Religious aspects--Christianity. 3. Miracles. I. Title.
 BV4400.S45 2013
 231.7′3--dc23

                                                                        2013007724

P 23 22 21 20 19 18 17 16 15 14 13 12 11 10 9 8 7 6 5 4

Y 33 32 31 30 29 28 27 26 25 24 23 22 21 20 19 18 17

Contents

A Note About Reading This Book

It's quite something to write a book about doing supernatural things. It's a little out there. I'm acutely aware of this.

In fact, it's often seemed to me that supernatural ministry is the most countercultural thing there is. It's not just unusual by social standards; it actually runs counter to the entire natural world as we typically experience it. This means that anyone who gets involved with supernatural ministry is probably going to end up with an unusual personal story line. And that, I'm here to tell you, is definitely part of the challenge.

So, while this book is largely meant to be instructional, I've also tried to make it personal in hopes of encouraging the personal journeys of those who read it. One of the ways I've tried to make it personal has shaped the book's organization.

You'll notice that the chapters come in an alternating sequence. Before each instructional chapter, I've inserted a mini-chapter containing nothing more than a story from my own life. In each instance, the story will relate in some way to the subject of the subsequent chapter. I did it this way so I could share personal stories without having to complicate the instructional chapters with a lot of lengthy anecdotes. I do include very brief stories in the instructional chapters, but they're simply used to illustrate points, whereas the longer stories are more about characterizing different supernatural ministries. I want to explain supernatural ministries, but I also want to try to give you a little feel for them, and, more particularly, to give you a feel for what it's like to grow with them.

It's hard to pursue supernatural ministry without it changing you, and you can't engage it without encountering loads of new challenges and questions as you go. Ideally—to introduce what will be a theme—*supernatural ministry will do a lot to make you a supernatural person*, which is a heck of a thing. I share stories and lessons that reflect ways in which this process has developed for me and those around me. It's my fondest hope that you, as an honest traveler, will acquire a lot of good stories of your own.

Because my short storytelling chapters lead into the instructional ones, and because successive instructional chapters build on preceding content, it's pretty important that you read the chapters in the order in which they're presented.

All the stories I share in this book are true, but I have occasionally changed names or inconsequential details in order to protect people's privacy or security.

What Miracles Are Like

There were about sixty-five of us wedged into a sweltering house church in a withered, bomb-blast of a neighborhood in Santiago de Cuba. "This is a place no American ever sees," my Cuban friend assured me. It was a barrio of deeply cratered streets, rusted hulks of cars, crumbling cement houses, starving dogs and knots of staring, shirtless men with bottles of liquor. For political reasons, foreigners aren't usually allowed to preach in communist Cuba, so to keep the informants at bay, I just shared a semiformal greeting with the church and closed by prayerfully asking the Holy Spirit to do something powerful for the congregation. Then it got kind of interesting.

Moved by the Spirit, one of the pastors of the church stood up to prophesy with her baby boy nursing at her breast. She spoke boldly of the purposes of God for her city. She spoke stirringly of the purposes of God for her church. And as her prophecy rose to poetic passion, her kid peed triumphantly all over the floor. She grabbed a mop in the corner to sop the mess and completed her prophecy with the mop held aloft in one arm, the suckling boy in the other, like a lactating Lady Liberty. The crowd broke into praise.

My team of three young Americans took the cue and began ministering to the sick, laying hands on their shoulders, eyes, ears and stomachs. We began to see healings. A man's fever disappeared. A woman with painful arthritis in her knees could suddenly walk without her cane. Another sick woman in the line was overcome by supernatural power during the prayer and, as happens a lot, fell unconscious, but my inexperienced teammate had never seen anything like that and assumed he'd somehow hurt her: "Oh God! Lady, lady, you're okay! Wake up, please! Señoooooraaaaa!"

On my other side, the two young women on our team watched another lady faint under the power of the Spirit, and as they prayed for her, a curious little mound rose from under the skin on her flat belly. When they touched the bump, it observably moved around to different parts of her abdomen. This unsettled them.

"Jordan," one of them whispered to me urgently, "do you think it's a demon?"

I sensed an opportunity for sarcasm. "Tell me, do you have any other theories for the freakish moving lump?"

They didn't.

"Then maybe you want to try casting it out."

They hurriedly discussed the idea and tried it. The bump disappeared and the lady woke up.

For my part, I rebuked the spirit of addiction in a suffering young man standing in front of me, and the fine fellow proceeded to vomit on the one pair of shoes I'd brought with me on the trip. Then, after a few moments, he opened his eyes wide, grinned brilliantly and praised God, having immediately sensed the profound change of deliverance. I patted his back and slipped out of my sneakers.

People in the street heard the general ruckus, and one suspicious passerby bravely shoved his way inside to look around. Three of the worshipers immediately surrounded the young tough, grabbed his shoulders and began praying. The guy simply burst into sobs and, without discussion, asked God into his life.

We continued like that for a long while, sweating like wrestlers, and eventually I leaned against a wall to take it all in: bodies on the floor in spatters of urine and vomit, drunks jeering through the windows, demons manifesting eerily, babies whining for the breast, a woman's crippling pain disappearing, fevers breaking, hearts changing—the weeping, the singing, the stretched faces of poverty and the shocking messiness of God's presence with humans. And somewhere in the mix of the grit and glory, the wonder and the wretchedness, I managed to have one crystal thought: This is what miracles are like.

Introduction

Supernatural People

It would be hard for me to say what the best part of supernatural ministry is, but I'll tell you what I think the most beautiful part is. It's the messiness.

In heaven, miracles would seem totally natural. Only on earth does it make sense to talk about things being supernatural. It's precisely because supernatural things are coated in earthly grit that they seem other-than-natural to us. By definition, they're out of place. They're like heaven in a brown paper bag. They're messy.

As a result, supernatural phenomena on earth might not even seem heavenly at first. We see this in the Gospels. Religious critics who saw Jesus' miracles up close frequently complained that they were dark and unlawful. They just didn't seem transcendent enough. And I can see how that might have been—what with the disorderliness of the crowds, the screaming of the exorcised demons, the healings that violated sabbath customs, and the strain that must have shown on Jesus' face as, we're told, he sometimes lacked the time to eat or experienced such exhaustion that he could sleep in a tiny boat pitching violently on a raging sea. Jesus did things that were unmistakably powerful, but they often seemed as odd as they did impressive, and this stayed true until the end. He healed multitudes, but lived as a beggar and died as a criminal. He was miraculous, but also gritty. He was, in a word, supernatural.

I think this messiness was by design. The character of God isn't really shown by his power; it's shown by the combination of his power and his vulnerability. Yes, he's all-powerful, but he suffers with you. Yes, he's Lord, but he won't lord it over you. If he were merely wondrous, he'd be unreachable, but he's also lowly, so you can trust him. The revelation is in the messy mix.

It seems to me that those of us who follow Jesus should try to be supernatural in the same rich way that he was. This means, on the one hand, that we should walk in God's miracle-working power as Jesus did. Jesus said, "These signs shall accompany believers: In my name they will drive out demons; they will speak in new tongues; they will pick up snakes and drink deadly poison without being hurt; they will place their hands on sick people and make them well" (Mark 16:17-18). He told us to pray that God's "kingdom come . . . on earth as it is in heaven," and where heaven reigns, one expects to see signs of heaven's power. "If I drive out demons by the Spirit of God," Jesus said, "then the kingdom of God has come upon you" (Matthew 12:28, my translation). The apostle Paul agreed that "the kingdom of God is not a matter of talk but of power" (1 Corinthians 4:20). "My message and preaching were not with wise and persuasive words," he said, "but with a demonstration of the Spirit's power" (1 Corinthians 2:4-5).

On the other hand, it means that as we move in supernatural power, we should also embrace a supernatural life—an other-than-natural, strange-looking life, marked by all of humanity's vulnerability and grit. To walk in Jesus' power, we should live in his lowly lifestyle. God's healers should place themselves among the needy, his deliverers among the desperate, his prophets among those in dark places, and they should share the burden of the suffering they find. If we want miracles, we should live the sort of life in which they're needed.

The supernatural ministries we're going to talk about in this book—ministries like healing, deliverance and prophecy—aren't just meant to show God's might; they're

If we want miracles, we should live the sort of life in which they're needed.

meant to show God's nature, which, again, is a mix of both power and humility. If your image of supernatural ministry is one of above-it-all transcendence, or if it's heavily characterized by preening miracle workers on a spot-lit stage, then perhaps you've been misled.

Jesus warned, "Many will say to me on that day, 'Lord, Lord, didn't we prophesy in your name and in your name drive out demons and in your name perform many miracles?' Then I will tell them plainly, 'I never knew you'" (Matthew 7:22). We need to remember that the real goal of any miracle is to deepen love with God. I think this is one reason God's kingdom is set up in such a way that we can't work effectively in supernatural power without sacrificing as we do it—because sacrifice is the truest expression of love.

So, before getting to the ministry-specific, how-to chapters of this book, I thought I'd discuss some ways in which supernatural ministry helps us to become supernatural people—wonderfully messy people with a healthy disregard for normal living. In particular, we'll talk about how supernatural ministry helps radicalize our outlook on life, and how it makes us disruptive in a good way that creates opportunities to reach people across boundaries. We'll also explore how it makes us highly vulnerable to painful situations, which is uncomfortable but transformative. Finally, we'll look at how supernatural ministry requires, and encourages, the faith to discover new things. Every supernatural minister is a pioneer of sorts.

Normal Weirdness

Supernatural ministry is weird by definition. The practice of healing, deliverance or prophecy can certainly feel weird as we do it. But I think the biggest problem among believers is not that we think supernatural ministries are too weird; it's that we try to make God seem normal.

Think about it. We believe in an invisible being with no beginning who spoke the universe into existence; who lives outside space and time with fantastic angelic creatures; who is everywhere and knows everything and can do anything; who sent his God-man Son into our world, brought him back to life after he was thoroughly killed, and then returned him to heaven; and who resurrects us so we can live forever. Once you swallow all that overwhelmingly supernatural stuff, it's only the tiniest step to accept supernatural healings and demonic deliverances—one drop in a whole bucket of weird.

No one who believes in God is entitled to reject supernatural ministries simply because they seem strange. But there's something in all of us that isn't comfortable being weird. We crave a respectable God-experience. So, we're apt to manage our emphases.

We emphasize Bible study instead of experiencing and doing the stuff in the Bible stories.

We focus on our church experience instead of our kingdom mission, and on our careers instead of our calling.

We're comfortable talking about Christian ethics, but hesitant about the idea of real interactions with a present God.

One nice thing about supernatural ministries is that they can help us stop pretending we're normal. There's little chance of us feeling normal when we're trying to cast a demon out of someone or trying to talk our way into the ICU to lay healing hands on a car crash victim. Such experiences remind us that we're weird, and this can be really helpful for spiritual living.

Anyone who is strange enough to cast out demons is going to have an easier time thinking about finances, relationships and life goals in ways that are "not of the world" (John 17:16). If you're unusual enough to try to heal people supernaturally, then you'll probably have less trouble being supernaturally generous with the poor or with disrupting your life to reach the unreached. If you accept that you can do even the supernatural things that Jesus and his followers did in the Gospel stories, then you've pulled a linchpin: If you can do Jesus' miracles, then you can live Jesus' lifestyle across the board. In this way, supernatural ministry reinforces kingdom living. The supernatural begets the radical.

I started thinking about this after noticing how Jesus himself used supernatural ministry to radicalize his followers. For example, the first time Jesus sent out his disciples without him, he gave them authority and instructions to "heal the sick, raise the dead, cleanse those who have leprosy, drive out demons" (Matthew 10:8). He also forbade them to take along food, money or extra clothes for their journeys (Matthew 10:9-10). In other words, he forced them to rely entirely on supernatural power.

Presumably, the residents of the villages they visited would provide for their needs because the disciples would be performing life-changing miracles in their midst. But if the disciples failed to work the miracles they'd been ordered to try, they would go hungry. The villagers would have found them absurd. Jesus' disciples either pulled off miracles or they suffered immediate and grave personal consequences. The advantage of this exercise was that when the disciples got used to relying on supernatural power—to doing the otherworldly and impossible—it became much more difficult to intimidate them. Neither sickness nor demons nor social awkwardness nor material need had much hold. It was a supernatural boot camp, and we all probably need something like it.

Believers should be attracted to impossible situations like frat boys to beer. We should be drawn to every warzone, disaster area, cancer ward, violent ghetto, impoverished people or unreached group. Wherever the world has no solution, the believers should rush in. Why? Because God makes all things possible. But being unafraid takes practice. Sometimes a situation is so bad that it seems like it will take a miracle to do any good, but this won't seem like such a big deal if you're actually used to supernatural things. We won't ever get all the miracles we want, but even the potential of supernatural breakthrough makes us a lot harder to frighten.

> Wherever the world has no solution, the believers should rush in. Why? Because God makes all things possible.

My friendship with Heidi, a young mother in our church, started when I prophesied some things to her about God raising her up to be a leader. Over the years we served together on our church's healing team and witnessed the supernatural cure of cancer patients, severe depressives and one particularly precious boy who couldn't walk. Heidi is soft spoken and dresses conservatively, but during our forty-day fast for healing power over cancer, she shaved off her thick brown hair and went bald-headed in solidarity with the chemotherapy patients she prayed for.

A few years ago, Heidi came to tell me that she felt she'd received a supernatural vision from God instructing her to provide for the starving orphans of Swaziland, an AIDS-stricken African country she had just visited. We talked about how anyone, let alone a shy mother with no significant resources, could provide for thousands of orphans in a desperately poor country. In the end, I shrugged and said, "Well, I guess you'll need a miracle." She just chuckled and nodded. Today, Heidi's organization has developments in three Swaziland locations, and her teams in Africa have seen supernatural healings of several severe diseases.

"Something funny happened to me when I shaved my head," she says. "Whatever it was, I think it led to this whole Swaziland thing." The pursuit of supernatural power had made her wonderfully weird.

Many believers have accomplished wonderful work for God without practicing ministries such as healing, deliverance or prophecy. But if you're looking for a way to multiply fearless choices or to disciple a whole community of believers in radical faith, I think you'd do well to take a page from Jesus' playbook and encourage supernatural ministries. It might seem weird, but there's a kind of weirdness that should be normal for believers.

Disruption

Even if you're comfortable being weird, there's always a chance that your supernatural activities will make other people uncomfortable with you. By definition, supernatural things are status-quo shakers. They shock and disrupt. This can be challenging in some settings, but an immense blessing in others. So you'll need to became good at applying the disruptions well.

When I was in my early twenties and exploring different church ministries, a successful area pastor wanted to impress upon me the danger of rejection and controversy. He sat me down and warned me gravely, "That Holy Spirit stuff just freaks people out! It can confuse people. You're better off without it."

But, I remember thinking, can a ministering believer ever really escape rejection and controversy? It's wise to be sensitive about how supernatural healings, deliverances or prophecies can shock people, but we have to be sensitive about all forms of ministry, don't we? Some people get offended when they hear preaching, but we don't question whether we should preach; we just think about when and how to do it.

I think supernatural ministries should work the same way.

In the Gospels we see that Jesus sometimes preached, sometimes healed and often did both. In Acts, we see that Paul simply preached and debated in Athens, but employed "extraordinary miracles" in Ephesus. He coached the Corinthians to practice supernatural ministries "intelligibly," with special attention given to "the unbeliever or those who do not understand," so that even the uninitiated would ultimately "fall down and worship God, exclaiming, 'God is really among you!'" (1 Corinthians 14:25).

The point is to have the right ministry tool for every situation and to apply it well. The special advantage of supernatural ministries is that they create opportunities in situations where "normal" methods don't seem to be working.

My church's healing services often attract people who would never come to hear a sermon. They come when they're sick, though, because they've heard some unusual stories of healing. In fact, sometimes miracles can be a kind of sermon. As when Jesus told his critics, "I have authority to forgive sins," and then told the paralytic lying there, "Get up, take your mat and go home" (Mark 2:1-12), a healing can send a very effective message. So too, our healing ministry often provides messages of God's grace to people before we even say a word about it.

In a similar way, supernatural experiences sometimes become fodder for provocative and unconventional testimonies. I think of my friend Greg who, after a supernaturally dramatic entrance into the kingdom, shared disarmingly at his baptism in front of all the friends he invited, "All I can say is, Jesus changes things. Like, if you've never been delivered from a demon, I highly recommend it!"

One of the great advantages of supernatural ministries is the way they can help us disrupt cultural barriers. If a person in another country hears me give an accurate prophecy about him, it's especially evocative, because cultural or linguistic divides normally would preclude my knowing anything about him. Similarly, a few years ago in Bangladesh, several American women on our team suddenly and supernaturally found themselves able to pray fluently (albeit temporarily) in the local Bangla language. It was a shocking—and very encouraging—sign to the locals.

> Supernatural ministries can help us disrupt cultural barriers.

In some of the foreign places I travel, witch doctors control villages by performing various supernatural feats. In these places, if I can't show God's power over sicknesses or demons, I'm not considered worth listening to. So, it's typical for our teams to begin by asking the village chief for permission to pray for sick people. After a healing or two, we ask to share a message. In these cases, supernatural ministry is a matter of establishing credentials.

In other situations, supernatural ministries just accomplish much more much faster than natural means could. Several years ago, in a small Cuban pueblo with no church, our team prayed for a woman dying of liver disease. She was the matriarch of the only Christian family in town, and she had been sent home from the hospital with no hope. Her skin was jaundiced, and the whites of her eyes had turned a bright, sickly yellow. She bowed her head as we laid hands on her, and when she lifted her face, we immediately noticed that her eyes were no longer yellow. A worker coming in from the fields happened to pass at that moment and, seeing the event, asked questions. Within minutes he was praying to ask God to enter his life. On a subsequent trip a year later, we confirmed that the woman had been permanently healed, that news of it had spread throughout the area and that a growing body of believers was meeting in the woman's home.

Sometimes, even if seekers fail to receive a miracle, they still find God in the attempt. Five years ago, an elderly Buddhist woman who had never been inside a church came to one of our healing services in hopes of a cure for her total blindness. When I laid hands on her eyes, we got an encouraging sign: she said she seemed to see lights. Nevertheless, after some time, she showed no progress, and I had to send her home with a promise to try again later. The next week she came back to our worship service, handed me a box of cookies she had baked, and told me the story of what happened after the healing service.

As she prepared for bed that night, she said, she felt a presence in her room, and when she turned toward it, she suddenly could see perfectly. She saw a man standing there. "I knew it was Jesus," she told me, "even though I had never seen him before." She said, "We talked for hours, all night long, about this and that." Eventually Jesus said it was time for him to go. "When he walked out the door, I suddenly couldn't see any more."

The woman expressed no disappointment about being cured only temporarily. "I just wanted to come back this week and tell you that I believe now," she assured me, patting my hand. "I know Jesus, and I'm not scared anymore." The cookies were chocolate chip; she brought me several batches over the months, until she passed away.

A tribal woman is healed of tumors in the mountains of Thailand. A crippled three-year-old walks in Sri Lanka. An African villager is healed of lung disease. An apparently insane villager in northern Bangladesh recovers his mind after young missionaries lay hands on him. A crippled neuropathy sufferer dances in Honolulu. In all these instances, supernatural ministry made a way for us when natural pathways seemed closed. Jesus said, "You will receive power when the Holy Spirit comes on you; and you will be my witnesses . . . to the ends of the earth" (Acts 1:8). If we're to spread God's love all over the world, in every kind of situation, then we have to be disruptive.

Supernatural ministry expands the options available to us.

Vulnerability

For me the most transformative part of working with supernatural ministries probably has had less to do with their strangeness and more to do with their emotional weight. Any seasoned Jesus follower will tell you how important it is to be in touch with your own weakness and to have seasons in which you're compelled to cry out desperately for God. Such experiences stretch our faith and mature our hearts. They're also awfully uncomfortable; we mostly try to avoid them. But supernatural ministry makes them hard to avoid.

Once you start pursuing supernatural ministries, you'll be exposed to more heartbreaking situations than you might otherwise see. If you're successful at your ministry, desperate people will begin searching you out. They'll show up at your church or call you to deathbeds. You'll spend more time in hospitals and drug treatment centers.

To complicate matters, supernatural ministries break down some of the emotional barriers we use to protect ourselves from other people's pain. Physicians care for many suffering people, but they reach a point at which they can say with confidence, "I've done all I can." Supernatural ministers, however, don't have a clear stopping point. Theoretically, nothing is impossible for us with God, and so there's no situation from which we're automatically excused. A supernatural life has few fences for shelter.

If you believe God enables you to perform supernatural feats, you'll sometimes feel terrible when you fail. At our church's healing services, roughly half of those who come for ministry receive at least partial physical healing during the service. Many experience progressive healing afterward, and about 15 percent receive total and immediate healing during the service itself. We register about a 10 percent success rate even with ostensibly incurable diseases. We seem to have an almost perfect success rate with some diseases, and our breakthrough rate for deliverance ministry is also quite high. We're in no way approaching Jesus' level of power and effectiveness, but I guess you could say there's cause for encouragement. Yet when we fail to heal a beautiful little girl with leukemia or a young mom with brain tumors, we feel the bite, and almost always wonder if we should have done better.

"Why couldn't we cast the spirit out?" the disciples asked Jesus after failing to help a very sick little boy. Jesus answered, "Because you have so little faith," and added, "This kind only comes out through prayer and fasting" (Mark 9:14-29, my translation). In other words, Jesus suggests that the disciples could have done the miracle but failed due to their poor preparation. That's very unnerving! It means we might actually share responsibility for the crushing disappointments that sometimes accompany miraculous ministry. And that means we have to get used to resting truly in God's mercy and grace, which takes far more maturity than just pretending there's nothing we could have done in the first place.

Supernatural ministries might also complicate some of your relationships. Sometimes hurting people actually will get angry at you if you don't deliver a miracle. And if your fellowship becomes known for supernatural ministries, more desperate people will show up, which could create social pressures. Your church partners might have to get comfortable worshiping next to advanced AIDS sufferers wheezing into oxygen tanks or delusional schizophrenics undressing in the corner during Bible study (oh, the stories I could tell). If you heal a homeless man of mental illness or addiction, you'll still have to deal with his homelessness. If you cast evil spirits out of people, you might still have to contend with the problem behaviors that led to their trouble. You have to think about how to make your church accessible to struggling people, and some of your churchmates might chafe at the changes.

Most fundamentally, supernatural ministry might complicate your relationship with God. If we believe God empowers miracles, then we'll have occasion to wonder why he doesn't just sovereignly come through for us when we're not getting the particular miracle we really want. It opens us to disappointment and to subsequent doubts about God's compassion. I have what I think is a pretty clear theological understanding about why God tends to not just drop miracles from the sky (we'll discuss it later). But though I can explain away my disappointments, I frequently don't have the strength of heart to weather them well. Sometimes I cry out to God for help, but sometimes I just scream. Often I do both.

Even if we navigate all these challenges, there's still one more blow: we'll find that even very successful supernatural ministry doesn't solve everything. The Lord might empower me to heal someone of cancer today, but that person will die of something eventually. I might cast a demon out of someone, but, as Jesus once pointed out, if the person doesn't eliminate his sinful vulnerabilities, demons can infest again. I might even visit some deprived village and raise a child from the dead, but that wouldn't solve the village's deadly poverty. Even when miracles should change a soul, they don't always: Jesus healed ten lepers on the road, but only one came back to acknowledge him. Miracles are awesome, but people are fickle. It's common to underestimate the value of supernatural ministries, but it's also possible to want them to accomplish too much.

> Miracles are awesome, but people are fickle.

I've got a couple good reasons for being frank about all these challenges. One, it's good to be prepared for them. Two, I think it's good to appreciate their worth. There are all sorts of Christian ministries that should expose us to hurting people and painful situations, but supernatural ministry has a unique way of driving us toward weakness, of ensuring we feel vulnerable. You can preach excellent weekly sermons at a church or administer some charity and still manage to hang around only happy, convenient people. But to have an excellent healing or deliverance ministry, you'll have to deal deeply and directly with the suffering, and you'll feel the weight of it. It's hard to carry that weight without the benefit of an intense fellowship with Jesus. That's the good part. If you're consistently embracing desperate people, and if you're pushing through related disappointments, then you'll have to confront your own selfishness, and you'll have to pursue the Lord passionately or your ministry will simply die out. It comes with the terrain.

Renewal

One final thing that supernatural ministry may require of you is what you might call the faith to discover—or to rediscover, as the case may be.

I'm often asked this sort of question: if supernatural ministries are so useful and have been as prevalent as many claim, then why don't all churches and traditions use them today? It's a good question that actually reflects a profound historical reality. The truth is, while supernatural ministries have been both common and enormously fruitful in church history, they've never been what you could call steady. Over the centuries we see great renewals of supernatural ministry followed by long droughts of disuse. It's up and down, here then there, a consistent inconsistency. You can focus on regional revivals and conclude that supernatural ministries have been constant, but you could just as well focus on down times and conclude that supernatural ministries ended with the first apostles. Really, it's the variation that needs explaining. Why do supernatural ministries surge so often only to dwindle so frequently?

Since supernatural ministries have never been entirely absent, it's hard to argue that God decided to stop empowering them, so the cause for variation must lie with us. My theory is this: groups of believers frequently figure out how to do supernatural ministry, but they have a hard time figuring out how to live with the ministry. Revivals come with great exhilaration and fruitfulness; downturns come when people tire of the level of weirdness, vulnerability and sacrifice that supernatural ministry demands.

One result of this variation is that very few believers have had the benefit of what you could really call a tradition in supernatural ministries, so each new generation has to do the work of rediscovering the ministries for themselves.

It's always been this way. For example, the use of supernatural ministry by first-century believers is well-chronicled in Scripture and elsewhere, but by the late second century the church father Irenaeus in his *Against Heresies* actually had to reassure his readers that supernatural works were still practiced fruitfully in his jurisdiction. "For some do certainly and truly drive out devils," he wrote. "Others have foreknowledge of things to come: they see visions, and utter prophetic expressions. Others still, heal the sick by laying their hands upon them, and they are made whole. Yea, moreover, as I have said, the dead even have been raised up, and remained among us for many years."[1]

In the next century the seminal theologian Origen wrote from Alexandria of "traces of that Holy Spirit" among Christians who "expel evil spirits and perform many cures, and foresee certain events," but it was only "traces."[2] A century later, in the same city, Bishop Athanasius extensively documented the miracles of his Egyptian contemporary, Anthony of the Desert, but his whole project was based on the notion that only exceptional monks were doing such ministry.[3]

The great Augustine of Hippo totally dismissed the possibility of supernatural ministries initially, but then he encountered them during a fifth-century revival in his native North Africa. In the last section of *The City of God* he offers gushing accounts of healings, concluding "even now miracles are wrought in the name of Christ."[4] He reportedly collected accounts of recent miracles for pastors to read aloud in the churches he supervised in order to rekindle the ministries.

We have rather detailed accounts of the use of supernatural ministries by Patrick, Columba and other monk evangelists of the western European outreach.[5] In a wonderfully personal letter to Augustine of Canterbury in A.D. 601, Gregory, bishop of Rome, acknowledged the use of miracles to attract English natives to Christ, and even offered advice for handling the pressures of being a supernatural minister.[6] But by the later middle centuries, as central church leaders focused on governance rather than outreach, supernatural ministries seem to have survived only on the fringes.

Early Reformation leaders strenuously dismissed miracle stories as a ploy by Catholics to legitimate their dominance, but it didn't take long for Protestant pioneers to rediscover the usefulness of supernatural tools. Scottish Reformers John Knox, Alexander Peden and George Wishart had highly regarded prophetic ministries in their day. (Wishart even predicted his own murder.) John Welsh, a leading Reformer at the turn of the seventeenth century, was recognized as a man of "prophetic utterance" and was credited with raising a man from the dead.[7] Seventeenth-century biographers of reform clergyman Robert Bruce systematically collected eyewitness accounts of the many healings, deliverances and other supernatural manifestations linked with his evangelistic meetings.[8]

And yet less than a century later, the great British revivalist John Wesley was shocked to find "that signs and wonders are even now

wrought by his holy child Jesus."[9] His revered journals are spiced
with accounts of deliverances and healings, and also of the oppo-
sition he experienced from "formal, orthodox men [who] began
even then to ridicule whatever gifts they had not themselves and to
decry them all as either madness or imposture."[10] Wesley's New
England contemporary, Jonathan Edwards, often called the dean of
American theology, wrote some of his most ardent essays to fend off
Christian critics who didn't trust the supernatural manifestations
that characterized his revival ministry.[11] Even his wife was called to
defend what she called her "joyful views of divine things."[12]

Francis Asbury, the first American Methodist bishop, was so passionate about supernatural ministry that he used to command his
preaching protégés to "Feel for power, feel for power!" Two Methodists and a Presbyterian touched off the Cane Ridge Revival on the
American frontier in the early 1800s—a movement that popularized
the phrase "slain in the Spirit." But today few Methodists or Presbyterians are aware of this movement, and neither of those denomina-
tions is known for practicing supernatural ministry.

Supernatural ministries played a big role in the establishment of
the early church, the birth of monasticism, the expansion of the faith
to Western Europe, the spread of the Reformation, the great revivals
of the Atlantic and American frontier evangelism. And yet in each
instance, practitioners had to discover it anew for themselves.

So, what does this pattern of atrophy and rediscovery mean
for you?

Well, it means that while you may or may not have had some supernatural experiences with the Lord, you probably haven't benefited from a lot of examples of living with supernatural ministries. If
you're at a church that practices supernatural ministry, the church is
probably relatively new to it. And even if your church does have a
strong supernatural tradition, chances are the congregation has ex-

perienced some dramatic waxing and waning in the effectiveness of its supernatural ministries. In all, if you're interested in supernatural ministries, it's likely that you're in a place of rediscovery or renewal, and that requires a certain sort of faith.

There's a style of Christian discipleship that is conservative, in the literal sense of the word: its emphasis is on preservation, affirming what's proven and familiar. There's another sort of discipleship that presumes new things and experiences—not liberal, in the sense of giving license to violate the old or established, but progressive, in the sense of Jesus' teaching on "new wineskins" for "new wine." To embrace all the works of the kingdom, we have to be willing to expand our containers of knowledge and experience. To pursue supernatural ministry, we need the faith for this progressive sort of discipleship. We have to be willing to try things, to reach for things we've only heard of, to explore and discover, to act without being totally sure how to act. Supernatural ministry entails adventure.

A Question of Heart

An insightful pastor once told me over dinner after I did a seminar at his church, "Honestly, this all scares me. I saw the people get healed, and I can't argue biblically with what you said. But I know what this would mean for us, and I'm not sure we're ready."

What is it worth enduring to be supernaturally powerful people? What's it worth to see the sick healed, the oppressed delivered or the miraculous manifest? It's a great question, one that you'll probably have to consider. People often seem to think that the big questions

> The one-two rhythm of the kingdom is
> power and meekness, strength plus vulnerability,
> authority with humility, glory and grit.

surrounding supernatural feats have to do with whether they're even possible today, but I think the more important questions always have to do with how difficult they are. And ultimately, those are questions for the heart.

Kingdom work has always been more about devotion than expertise, and the pursuit of God's empowerment always draws us into God's heart. He's never satisfied with a mere show of power when he can also demonstrate his lowliness and love. So, the one-two rhythm of the kingdom is power and meekness, strength plus vulnerability, authority with humility, glory and grit. This is why supernatural power requires other-than-natural living. It's why miracles are messy things. Here's hoping God messes up your life.

You Do It

A few years ago I received half an invitation to speak at a large, enormously wealthy church in California. I say it was half an invitation because once it was offered, the church's staff split angrily over whether or not to let me come.

The issue wasn't that they doubted my ministry, but that they didn't. Some staffers were worried, about how their sensitive church members would react if I actually succeeded at doing something supernatural. People might think it was too weird.

At first the invitation was simply withdrawn, but ultimately the staff negotiated a compromise. I was told I could give a sermon, but I was ordered not to "pray for the Holy Spirit to come upon the crowd," lest it cause somebody to faint or do something strange. I could talk about supernatural ministry, but I wasn't to do any healing or deliverance or prophecy—unless maybe people approached me privately and discreetly after the service.

In essence, I couldn't ask God to manifest because, you know, he might actually do it, and in doing it he might take too many liberties. I think maybe God's social skills were in question.

The terms were so fascinating that I just had to go and see what would happen. During my sermon I described supernatural ministry and how I experience it practically. For the sake of illustration, I said, "Hey, is there anyone here with, say, really bad knee problems that make it hard to walk?"

Five good-natured people raised their hands.

"Well, OK, if I were going to try healings today, I would simply say, 'In the name of Jesus, knees be healed.'" Pause. "Then I might just ask you to check your knees, maybe by doing deep knee bends."

They were such fine sports that they went through the motions of flexing their joints. In the half minute we spent on this it became clear that four out of five of them were actually healed—including a young woman who was scheduled to have reconstructive knee surgery later that week. A little buzz broke out in the congregation. The reactions of the people whose knees had been healed ranged from blank stares to sudden tears.

"So yeah," I continued. "That's pretty much how we'd do supernatural ministry if we were going to do it." And I hurriedly moved on.

After the service, in a side wing of the church, people began approaching me, and before long we had about 125 people queued up to receive supernatural ministry, with dozens more lined up to watch. Some wanted healing, some wanted prophetic direction, and some just wanted me to pray that they might experience a supernatural touch from God. A couple of years later I found out that a person with abdominal cancer, who didn't even attend that church, wandered in, saw the scene, asked for prayer and was healed.

About three hours into the ministry time, a young woman asked for healing from the pain and immobility caused by a herniated disc in her back. In spite of her pain, she was chipper. "I didn't think I'd be doing anything like this today," she chuckled.

I said, "Hey, I'm getting pretty tired, so I'll make you a deal. If you get healed, you have to turn around and help heal the others." She gave me a dubious look, but agreed. "Great," I said. "Try touching your toes!"

She hesitated for just a moment, and then went for it like a trooper. And surprisingly enough, she found that she was suddenly pain free. She let out a bright yip, did a cute little happy dance and hugged a couple of her friends.

She was still laughing when I said, "OK, now you do it." The elderly man behind her had an arthritically frozen shoulder that prevented him from lifting his arm more than a few inches. The young woman cast a few sideways glances at her friends, but obligingly put her hand on the man's back and giggled, "Be healed in Jesus' name."

With a small jolt, the man's shoulder popped free. He raised his hand high, and then swung his arm in a circle—able to move the joint fully for the first time in years.

And at that point, the woman stopped laughing. Her face went pale, her eyes went wide, and she looked at me as if she were pleading for help. Her mouth was open but she couldn't speak. Finally she started weeping. "I don't know why I'm crying," she said. "I don't know why!"

Miracle Work

It's one thing to accept that supernatural stuff happens. It's another thing to accept it when it happens. It's still another thing to be the one through whom it happens.

This chapter is about getting used to the idea of being the one who actually does the supernatural stuff. I don't mean being someone who asks God for miracles, but rather being the person through whom the supernatural power flows—the person who lays hands on someone for healing, who gives commands of deliverance or who speaks the prophecy. And I don't simply mean being someone who performs miracles, but being someone who really works them—who does the hard work of preparation and application. The first practical key to doing supernatural ministry is to realize that you are the one who does it.

Depending on where you come from, this will either sound perfectly obvious or terribly sacrilegious. You might say, "Wait a minute! Only God can do miracles. It's wrong to say that we can do anything supernatural."

The reality is, God routinely partners with us to get things done in the world.

....

The first practical key to doing
supernatural ministry is to realize that
you are the one who does it.

....

He reveals truth, but we have to preach it.

He offers salvation, but we gather in.

He shows mercy, but we serve the poor.

Supernatural ministry works the same way: God is the source of the power, but we lay hands on people or speak commands that the power might flow to others. Who empowers supernatural feats? God. Who does them? We do, usually.

God certainly can perform miracles without our help. Think of the burning bush, or manna in the desert, or the sudden stars that led the magi. Yet it's usually his people who apply his power. Think of Moses lifting his staff to part the seas, or the elaborate administrations of the Israelites who circled Jericho. Think of Elijah stretching himself upon the dead widow's son, or Elisha stopping the waters of the Jordan by striking them with his mantle. Think of Jesus laying his hands on the lepers, or Peter and John giving the healing command to the paralytic at the gate, or Paul driving the demon from the slave girl in Philippi. There will occasionally be times when the Lord, according to the requirements of his purposes, manifests sovereignly in a place and simply makes supernatural things happen, but more often supernatural things happen because a mature minister has brought the power and moves in it.

Yet believers often think the best way to get miracles has something to do with convincing God to do them for us—maybe by asking him exceptionally well or with great confidence. Really, the question isn't how to convince God to do miracles for us, as if he were a fussy giver, but how to grow in the miracle-working power that God makes available to us. We shouldn't merely ask God to do miracles for us; we should work at performing them in his name. We shouldn't just pray, "Oh God, please heal John." We should be able to say, "John, in the name of Jesus, be healed!" We shouldn't just be miracle seekers; we should also be miracle workers.

To say that God works through us supernaturally is to say that supernatural stuff requires us to work at it. We have to prepare and exert ourselves when doing supernatural feats just as we have to prepare and exert ourselves in other sorts of ministries.

This point is foundational enough that I want to discuss it at some length. So I'm going to take a stab at explaining why God set up the world in such a way that kingdom ministry work is mostly done by us and not by him, and then I'll try to explain why supernatural ministries like healing, deliverance and prophecy are no different than other ministries in this respect. Then, I'll try to clarify the practical difference between seeking a miracle, on the one hand, and actually applying supernatural power, on the other. I'm hoping that by the end of the chapter, you won't just be eager for powerful supernatural things to happen, you'll be ready to go to work to get them.

Why Does Ministry Require So Much Work?

We all know that God leaves a lot of the ministry work of the kingdom to us. For instance, we know that God usually doesn't appear personally in the unreached corners of the world and preach evangelistic sermons; he uses us for that. God typically doesn't manifest in deprived places to feed the poor or dig wells; instead, he sends us. God partners with us to get things done.

The question is, why? It seems so inefficient. If God wants to provide excellent testimony about himself, he could cut out the middle man and do it alone. Why doesn't God just appear in the sky and make himself obvious to the world? If you think about it, this is probably the most obvious question for anyone exploring the existence and nature of God. If there is a God, why isn't he totally clear? Insofar as believers have a pat answer for this, it usually has to do with God's desire for us to accept things on faith. But, of course, that just raises another question: why does God require faith?

To answer that, I find it helpful to stress the distinction between believing that God exists and trusting that God is good.

Believing in the existence of God has never really been the main issue for us humans. Adam and Eve hung out in God's direct presence in the Garden. There were lots of friendly animals and everyone was naked, but it was cool—sort of like the Oregon commune where my mom lived when I was a teenager. But in spite of the idyllic conditions, the Deceiver convinced the innocent couple that God had prohibited the infamous fruit in order to oppress them. "God knows that when you eat of it you will become like God!" he said. And they bought the lie. The humans fully believed God existed, but they didn't trust his character. James reminds us that even the demons believe in God (James 2:19), but belief without trust is worthless.

You don't really trust something until you entrust yourself to it. You believe the rope bridge is there, but do you trust it to hold while you cross? You believe the deal is profitable, but do you trust your partner to keep his word? You believe God exists, but do you trust him to be there for you when you're actually on the line? To grow in trust requires real risks, real challenges.

> You don't really trust something until you entrust yourself to it.

And so I think God has gone out of his way to see that we all get some challenges. For one thing, God allows plenty of hardship in the world today. Perhaps Adam and Eve's life in the Garden was so perfect that they never had occasion to think about trusting God until they actually faced deception. Our situation is much different: the world's current suffering compels us to wrestle directly with the issue of God's kindness. Whereas Adam and Eve once believed in God without bothering to trust him, we have to grapple with his trustworthiness just to believe in his existence.

If general hardship weren't enough, I think God has also gone out of his way to ensure spiritual hardship. For example, have you ever wondered why there are demons in the world? Jesus and his gang drove out bunches of them, which showed God's power over demons, and Jesus' victory on the cross was certainly complete, so the dirty beasts can't possibly have any rights to the earth. So, why doesn't God just blink away the demons?

The situation reminds me of the story of the Israelites conquering the Promised Land. The tribes of Canaan had angered God with centuries of cruelty and other wickedness, and God empowered Israel to drive them out handily—but not completely. God left some tribes there, we're told, using them "to test all those Israelites who had not experienced any of the wars in Canaan (he did this only to teach warfare to the descendants of the Israelites who had not had previous battle experience): ... They were left to test the Israelites to see whether they would obey the [Lord]" (Judges 3:1-4). As if the hardscrabble difficulties of life were insufficient for developing trust, God arranged for his people to have some serious combat too.

In those early days, when God's people were starting out, the battles were against other humans, but as God's people matured through the centuries, our true adversaries became clearer. "Our struggle is not against flesh and blood," Paul tells the Ephesians, "but against the rulers, against the authorities, against the powers of this dark world and against the spiritual forces of evil in the heavenly realms" (Ephesians 6:12). These spiritual adversaries help guarantee that every follower of Jesus will have to fight hard.

Somehow in life, if we don't learn to fight, to risk it all, then we don't learn to trust well. So, God has not arranged a sit-back-and-relax kingdom. He's arranged a put-it-all-on-the-line kingdom. "The kingdom of heaven endures violence," Jesus said, "and it takes violent people to get a grip on it" (Matthew 11:12, my translation).

> God has not arranged a sit-back-and-relax
> kingdom. He's arranged a
> put-it-all-on-the-line kingdom.

In light of all this, it makes sense that the Lord would employ us for kingdom work on earth. Kingdom ministry, in effect, is the fight we need. In the same way God arranged for generations of Israelites to fight for their land, God has arranged for us to fight for ours. The sacrifices and hard work of ministry are the way we put ourselves on the line for Jesus. The exertion, the ridicule, the threats, the pain of ministry—these are the elements through which we fully entrust ourselves to a God we can't even see. In the life of faith, ministry is the thing that most often moves us from being mere believers to actual trusters.

The challenge of ministry is also an important way for us to model trust to the world. Anyone who puts him- or herself on the line for Jesus is making a statement about the Lord's character—about his worth and reliability. If we have to endure risk and sacrifice as we minister to the world, then the world sees trust in action. The messenger becomes part of the message.

I think that life is hard in order to develop trust in us, and ministry is hard in order to perfect and display it. Jesus warned his chosen apostles of rejection, persecution, imprisonment, torture and death.

The Lord said of the apostle Paul, "I will show him how much he must suffer for my name" (Acts 9:16). The most frequent command in the Gospels is "Don't be afraid!" Anyone who participates seriously in the progress of God's kingdom should expect some hard work, and there are good reasons for it to be this way.

Supernatural Ministries Are No Exception

So we understand that we're responsible to do the hard work of kingdom ministry. What we need to understand is that supernatural ministry is no exception. We shouldn't expect God to drop supernatural healings from the sky any more than we expect him to drop sermons from the sky. Instead, we should expect to work on each of them ourselves, and for God to empower us to do them both.

But while believers easily accept the idea that God has called us to do the work of preaching and teaching in the world, they sometimes have a harder time accepting the idea that we're called to do healing, deliverance or other supernatural ministries in the same direct fashion. When we encounter an individual looking for meaning in life, we don't just ask God to go talk to the person but rather go talk to him or her ourselves, but if we encounter someone suffering with physical disease, we'll pray that God would heal him or her rather than laying our hands on the person and saying, "Be healed!" In other words, we do our own preaching, but ask God to do the healing. We behave as if God would leave the administration of spiritual healing to us while reserving to himself the administration of the lesser miracle of a physical healing. It's a little odd when you think about it.

I'd guess that many believers are reserved about supernatural ministries simply because they aren't familiar with them. If we've never tried healing or deliverance, it can be easy to make exceptions of them. This is understandable, and the remedy is simple enough:

try some supernatural ministry and get some experience.

But I also suspect that some believers reject their role as hands-on supernatural ministers due to sincere concerns about, well, arrogance. Again, some think that since God is the source of all miracles, it would be irreverent for us to say that we can be miracle workers. For these believers it would seem perfectly fine for me to say, "I preached to someone today," but completely presumptuous for me to say, "I healed someone today."

I completely understand the sentiment, but there are a couple problems with the thinking.

First, it treats some ministries as human and some as divine, whereas, in truth, all ministries are both. In passages such as Romans 12 and 1 Corinthians 12 and 14, the Bible says that both teaching and healing are supernatural gifts from God. Wisdom, leadership, giving, helping and administration are all called "spiritual gifts," just as prophecy, tongues and "miraculous powers" are. There is no such thing as natural giftedness; it's all supernatural. (When you think about it, even life itself is a supernatural gift from God.) If we lead people well, it's a spiritual gift. If we preach or teach well, it's a supernatural phenomenon. And if we heal someone, cast out a demon or prophesy, that's also because of God's power. It all comes through God's Spirit, so it's a bad idea to treat some ministries as categorically differently from others.

The original apostles understood this because Jesus told them directly that God would empower even their preaching: "It is not you speaking," he said, "but the Holy Spirit" (Mark 13:11). When the apostles faced tough times, they knew to pray for divine power for both their preaching and their miracle working: "Enable your servants to speak your word with great boldness. Stretch out your hand to heal and perform signs and wonders through the name of your holy servant Jesus." And subsequently, "they were all filled with the

Holy Spirit and spoke the word of God boldly" (Acts 4:29-31), and "they performed many signs and wonders" (Acts 5:12). Preaching and miracle working—they were both considered part of the same supernatural fabric.

Of course, some ministries are more obviously supernatural than others, but that's not a categorical difference. It can be convenient to distinguish particular activities by calling them "supernatural ministries" (as I often do in this book), but this is a function of perspective or maybe a matter of degrees: we can try to preach "in the flesh" and pull it off in some limited fashion, but no one can begin to pull off a supernatural healing without actually relying on supernatural power (though fraudulent ministers might try to fake it). But again, this is not a fundamental difference. Though it might seem that preaching is human and healing is divine, the truth is that each is a combination: God empowers it; we employ it. Apart from God, I have no power to heal anyone of anything, but apart from God, I have no power to preach well either. So, if we're able to call ourselves preachers and leaders, we should certainly be able to think of ourselves as healers, deliverers and prophets.

The second big problem with exceptionalizing overtly supernatural ministries is that it can make us tragically passive and unprepared. For example, we know we shouldn't wait around for God to preach to the unreached, because that's our job. So, we pray about it and learn Scripture and study missiology and practice preaching like good soldiers. In a similar way, we shouldn't just wait around for God to heal the sick; we should lay hands on and heal them directly, and we should be working aggressively and diligently to become good healers. But if we convince ourselves that supernatural ministries should be left entirely to God, then we won't invest in preparing to do them, and then we'll be in no shape to try them when the time comes.

Preparation is a big deal. A good portion of this book is about what we can do to develop in God's power for supernatural ministries, because, as with most any ministry, the sacrifice of preparation is a large part of effectiveness. We understand that "normal" ministries like preaching require investment in terms of study, practice and focused prayer, but the need to prepare for overt supernatural ministries seems less understood. It's common for preachers to spend a full day or more preparing for their thirty-minute Sunday sermon, but I find far fewer pastors who do anything to prepare for, say, ministrations to the sick, even in cases in which such ministrations are included in their Sunday liturgy.

Many Christians don't even know they *can* prepare for ministries such as healing, deliverance or prophecy, and if we fail to understand that we should be working and investing in supernatural ministries, then we can develop a sort of fatalism where supernatural things are concerned. If we testify to a friend and fail to see him or her accept Jesus, we go home and pray about it and try again later, but if we pray to heal a sick friend and it doesn't work, we might say, "Well, I guess it's not God's will for so-and-so to be healed now." We interpret one outcome as a momentary failure in our ministry, but the other outcome as a function of divine destiny. This isn't sensible.

I'm reminded of my friend Nick who was part of a Bible study I led while finishing my postdoctoral work. Nick had been raised in church but fell hard into drugs and homosexual promiscuity. When he joined up with us, he wanted to get free of his excesses, but the struggle was fierce. One night he called me with bad news: he'd been diagnosed with HIV. "Well, Jordan," he said, "If God wants to heal me, I suppose he can."

"Of course he can," I said, "but we're going to get together to pray and fast and lay on hands, right?"

"No," he said, "I've just put it in God's hands. He can heal me in a moment if he wants to, so I'm just leaving it to him."

I argued gently with him for a bit, but he would have none of our hands-on healing because he had resolved in his mind that it was more appropriate "to submit to God's will for healing." Nick's passive attitude may partly have been a coping mechanism for dealing with the hurricane of emotions he was enduring. But it frustrated me to think that his church upbringing had given him no idea of the appropriateness of laboring together for supernatural healing. He believed God could do miracles, but he didn't believe in miracle ministry. By contrast, Nick had never said in our Bible study, "Well, if God wants to teach me, he can. It's in his hands." Instead, he actively worked his way into Scripture and openly received ministry from our teachers. It was only where supernatural ministry was concerned that he thought things should be left entirely to God.

A passivity toward supernatural things is all the more frustrating in that supernatural ministries, as a general rule, tend to require more investment and more active trust than other sorts of ministry. We already touched on this in chapter two: supernatural ministries tend to be very hard. So, if in addition to the inherent challenges we also convince ourselves that supernatural work isn't even something we should have to invest in, then we're doubly handicapped!

All this to say, while supernatural ministries might be exceptionally useful in many instances, they're not exceptional in other ways. We should treat them much the same as we treat other ministry tools. We should do the hard work of supernatural ministry just as we do the work of other ministries.

Petitions Versus Direct Ministry

Part of getting used to doing supernatural ministry is simply having a picture in our minds of how to go about doing it. In particular it's important to clearly appreciate the difference between petitioning and direct ministry. Instead of merely petitioning God to do miracles, we have to get comfortable applying his power ourselves.

To illustrate the difference: If your friend Trevor were desperately ill, you might ask God to heal him: "Oh God, please heal Trevor." You're petitioning God to heal your friend. As an alternative method, you could visit your friend in the hospital, lay a hand on his head and say, "In the name of Jesus, Trevor, be healed!" Instead of petitioning God to heal your friend, you're now using your own touch and your own words to release God's power into his body. This is a direct application.

In both cases we assume that all the power to heal originates with God, but the path of the ministry varies. When petitioning, you ask God to heal your friend, so the path goes from you through God to your friend. When ministering directly, God gives you power to heal your friend, so the path goes from God through you to your friend.

In petition you ask God to perform a healing. In direct application you perform a healing using God's power.

In petition you pray so that God would heal your friend. When ministering directly, you pray that God would give you power so that you can heal your friend.

Fortunately for us, God rarely makes a big deal about formulas, and it would be wrong to obsess about techniques. The truth is, I've seen useless legs healed following simple petitions to God, and I've also seen dysfunctional limbs healed by a believer's direct touch. I've known demons to manifest and exit an oppressed person after I asked Jesus to handle it, and I've also seen many demons flee when dismissed directly by believers. The exact method one uses in the moment of ministry is not necessarily a do-or-die issue.

However, when we remember that God desires us to be hands-on ministers, then it makes a lot of sense to try ministering directly. Plus, Scripture suggests that's how it should work.

In the many dozens of recorded episodes of supernatural healings in the New Testament, there is not a single case of a person being healed as the result of a petition alone. Every single recorded healing happens as the result of a person applying supernatural power directly to another person. In a few cases the minister initially petitions God to grant him or her power, but always the healing itself is triggered through a human touch, a spoken command, a transfer medium (like anointed cloths or oil) or some other form of person-to-person application. Demonic deliverances in Scripture follow this same pattern. It would be a mistake to make too much of this, but if I were pressed to lift from the pages of Scripture a model for doing miracles, I would have to emphasize applying miracles over petitioning for them.

But even if we fully accept that we're supposed to apply supernatural power directly, it can still be hard to get comfortable with it in practice, and sometimes our discomfort can be a bigger barrier than lack of understanding.

One thing that makes us uncomfortable when ministering directly is that it puts us on the spot. For instance, if we say, "Dear Lord, please heal my friend," then we're essentially putting the onus on God. If the healing fails, well, it's God's doing. But if we instead lay on a hand and say, "Brother, be healed in Jesus' name," then it puts the onus on us. It says to all onlookers that we're actually expecting something to happen right then and there, through our ministrations, and if nothing happens, we're left holding the bag. It feels like an actual, real-time test of whether we're filled with the Lord's power. There's far less wiggle room. It calls for a lot more trust than petitioning would—which is probably a big part of the reason God has us doing it this way.

Accordingly, around the ministry teams and training groups at our church, one of our most frequently used phrases is "You do it."

We use it as an encouragement. For example, if, during one of our small group ministry sessions, a young minister prays, "Dear Lord, my friend here is sick, so please come and heal her right now," one of our leaders will tap that minister on the shoulder and say, "OK, now you do it!" This is shorthand for "God heard you, but now try to apply some of the power God gives you." The young minister will stop petitioning God for intervention and instead put a hand on the sick woman and say, "In the name of Jesus, sister, be healed. Fever, go away!"

The same sort of thing might happen when a person requests prophetic guidance. A group of us will circle around the person, and a young minister might pray, "Dear Lord, my friend needs you to speak to him about his career choices, so please give him wisdom right away." Again, a leader might tap that minister on the shoulder and say, "Great, but now you do it," which means, "Be quiet and listen for a moment, and see if God doesn't give you a prophetic message to share with this person."

In saying "You do it," we're in no way trying to take focus off God. We're just trying to honor the way God has empowered us to minister. The point isn't really about the exact method we use, but it's a good idea for supernatural ministers to be comfortable with straightforward applications of God's power since the Lord is so committed to putting the power in our hands. "Heal the sick, raise the dead, cleanse those who have leprosy, drive out demons," Jesus ordered. "Freely you have received; freely give" (Matthew 10:8). What the Lord has given us, we freely share. What the Lord has given us to do, we try to embrace.

Growing in Ministry Power

At the beginning of the chapter I expressed a desire to make you eager to work on supernatural ministry, and if I've succeeded, then maybe you've begun to think about what kind of work might be involved.

If we think we should try to get supernatural things to happen just by asking God to grant them, then we'll try to motivate God. If, on the other hand, we embrace our role as direct supernatural ministers, then we'll work to develop the power God provides. This is an immense difference.

Jesus consistently makes clear that motivating God is not the issue: "Your father knows what you need before you ask," Jesus assures us (Matthew 6:8). He says, "If you then, though you are evil, know how to give good gifts to your children, how much more will your Father in heaven give the Holy Spirit to those who ask him?" (Luke 11:13). He promised, "You will receive power when the Holy Spirit comes on you" (Acts 1:8). God is already eager to give, and in particular, he's eager to give his Spirit to us that we might have more power to do the work of ministry.

> God is eager to give his Spirit to us that we might have more power to do the work of ministry.

So, where supernatural ministry is concerned, the question isn't whether God is willing to grant supernatural power to do it; it's what we can do to grow in that power.

This is the question we take up next.

Some Idea How

Toward the end of my freshman year at Stanford University, I started going to a church that practiced supernatural ministries. The first time people from that church prayed for me, they circled me and asked the Spirit to come. I promptly fainted and lay unconscious for about twenty minutes. This was different. And a bit disturbing.

Dramatic displays weren't my thing. Brooding intensity was my thing. I liked contact sports, poker and Hemingway short stories. The few social skills I had were built around being smart and self-controlled. Fainting did not figure into my personal idiom.

But I quickly did the cost-benefit analysis and decided that if fainting was the price to pay for experiencing more of God's manifest presence, then so be it. I started going to every church service or conference I could that might feature supernatural ministry. My prayer life expanded exponentially, and so did my experiences with the Spirit. Sometimes I'd ask for God's presence and I'd feel electricity in my body. Sometimes I'd have visions that were hard to describe. And then, lamentably, bewilderingly, appallingly, there was the fainting.

Once, during worship at a large gathering of Christian students from area colleges, I felt the telltale tingling of the Spirit's presence and scrambled behind some stacks of chairs before collapsing flat under what felt like a waterfall of power. I managed to get up about an hour later with no one having discovered me.

Another time I went with a group of about fifteen curious students from my campus fellowship to a supernatural ministry conference. At the end, when the conference leaders prayed for the Spirit to come upon the crowd, I was hit by a bolt of something and sank against a wall. When I came to, I was lying in the middle of the auditorium, completely alone in the room except for one unconcerned janitor sweeping around me. When I caught up to my friends, one of the senior students pulled me aside, patted my shoulder and gravely said, "I don't know what to say, Jordan. I just don't know."

I didn't really know either, and I wasn't always the best at explaining my experiences constructively. I'd never consistently been part of a Christian ministry until I got to college, and my campus fellowship was teaching me tons about Godly friendship and true, focused discipleship. But of the hundreds of young people in our fellowship, only a few had any sort of experience with supernatural manifestations.

My friend Paul had the most patience with me. Paul was a staff minister for my fellowship and a world-class encourager. The thing that made Paul great was that when I got excited about supernatural things, he explored with me. One night his roommate, Bill, got very sick with the flu. Paul waited until Bill was asleep and then crept beside his bed and prayed earnestly for an hour that he would be healed. I adored Paul for doing this. But the next morning, Bill was even sicker.

"I really wanted him to get better," Paul reported, "and I prayed very hard." He looked thoughtful. "I mean, did God not want Bill to get better?"

Some weeks later, our campus fellowship took a retreat at a mountain camp. It came at the end of an exam week during which I had exhausted myself by pulling a couple all-nighters, and apparently I had caught a virus. As I rode to the camp that day, I got so feverish that I shivered. I began to sweat profusely and turned alarmingly pale. I hated to miss anything, so when we all assembled into assigned groups that evening, I asked Paul if he would pray for my healing.

Paul gathered a few others to pray with us, then addressed the Lord reverently (Paul actually used words like *thee* and *thou*) and gently placed a hand on my back. I felt a surge of power shoot from his fingers, and I crumpled to the ground and was senseless for about five minutes, after which the fever was totally gone. In fact, I had so much energy that I stayed up all that night just for fun. But several in the group were upset with me because my fainting had seemed disruptive.

The next morning, I learned there had been a meeting of concerned leaders, and I was called in for "debriefing" with some of the staff.

"Well, Paul was the guy praying," I evaded. "Ask him what happened."

But they were more worried about me. Was I being mature? What was I going to do with these experiences? What did I think all these weird manifestations were for?

Eventually, Paul and I had a quiet talk, and I remember exactly what he said: "You, my friend, have a presence."

I didn't quite know what to make of that. "You mean I have God's presence, right? But don't we all have his presence?"

"Well, yeah," Paul answered, "but why do you think you got healed and not Bill? Does God love you more or something?"

We eventually concluded that was unlikely.

"The thing is," Paul continued, "it's hard for people to just plow into this supernatural stuff without having some idea how it works. How do you explain how it happens and then doesn't happen?"

I realized I had had some good experiences with the Spirit's man-ifest presence and power, but had almost no idea about what to do with those experiences. There had to be more to it than just the fainting, right? A person got filled with God's power so he or she could use that power, right? I thought of all I had learned that year about focused discipleship and growth, and something occurred to me. Surely, there must be some path of discipleship for supernatural stuff, too. Right?

"Maybe we're the problem, Paul," I said. "I mean, maybe God's totally willing to do the supernatural stuff, but there are things we should be doing to get stronger in it."

"OK, like what?" he said.

The Power Equation

This chapter is basically the heart of the book. It's where I tell you, as best I can, how to grow in power so you can do supernatural ministry more successfully.

But while I've made this a central part of the discussion, it seems to me that one could argue that it's rather unnecessary. Most believers would intuitively conclude that the best way to grow in God's power is simply to walk very closely with God, and I think they'd be right. To love the Lord, to submit to him, to serve others sacrificially, to imitate Christ in all ways—these are things that every follower knows to do, and, among other benefits, they're essentially the things that enable us to flow well in God's supernatural power. So, generally speaking, to become more supernaturally powerful, we'd do pretty well just by embracing deeply the things we already know, and nobody needs to read a whole chapter to understand that.

But there are a few big advantages to thinking about developing power in a way that's specific to doing supernatural ministries. For one thing, it's always helpful to have extra reasons to be mindful of the stuff we already know to do. For another, there's a happy reciprocity in it: if we walk closely with God, we'll grow in supernatural power, and if we invest in growing in supernatural power, we'll find ourselves walking more closely with God. Thinking about power development also helps shape the way we practice supernatural ministries. It encourages us to prepare specifically, and, as we'll see, it can also suggest helpful approaches to the moment of doing ministry.

But the most significant point about developing in God's power is simply this: growing in power is the biggest key to doing supernatural ministry well. It's crucial for every practitioner to understand this.

> The biggest key to doing supernatural ministry well is growing in power.

When I first started exploring supernatural ministries, I mistakenly thought the key to healing or delivering someone would be technical expertise—what to say, how to say it, whether to lay on hands, how to discern if a sickness has spiritual roots and so on. The books I found on supernatural ministries all seemed to stress methods: the five-step healing model, the proper way to identify and renounce a demon, the correct use of anointing oil. I came to believe that if I failed at a healing or deliverance, it was probably because I was executing it incorrectly. But in reality, method is not nearly as important as power. It's not even close. It's not so much what you say or do when you try to heal or deliver someone; it's how much power you have when you say or do it.

As an analogy, you might think of weightlifting. If you're trying to bench-press three hundred pounds, it will help a bit to know how to grip the bar properly and how to breathe effectively when you're lifting. But it will help you a heck of a lot more to have developed a lot of muscle.

So, we need to look at how to develop supernatural muscle, and fortunately the Bible has a fair bit to say about it.

The notion of growing in supernatural power is a common if sometimes subtle feature of kingdom stories and teachings. It started with the earliest accounts of kingdom ministry. For instance, after Jesus was baptized, the Spirit descended on him and he was "full of the Holy Spirit." But then "the Spirit led him into the wilderness" where he fasted and overcame temptation for forty days, after which "he returned to Galilee in the power of the Spirit" and began doing miracles (Luke 4:1-14). Notice the progression. Jesus already had the presence of the Spirit, but only after his spiritual work in the wilderness did he have the power of the Spirit. God's presence brings the power, but we actually have to do a little work to develop in that power for ministry. This applied to Jesus, so it certainly applies to us.

The Power Equation

To help us think about how to grow in supernatural power, I'm going to use a little device that I call the power equation. And just so you know, I'm totally embarrassed by the name of it.

It sounds so cheesy, like one of those lame money-making programs you see on late-night infomercials: "With the proven Power Equation™ system, you'll get out of debt now and earn thousands by working part time in your own home, all while melting inches off your waist!" The name also suggests a sort of mathematical precision that doesn't really apply. But I'm going with it because the concept of an equation actually helps to illustrate how several different elements can combine together to increase our power in the Spirit.

Plus, a little embarrassment is probably good for the soul.

So, here's the power equation in all its glory:

Authority + Gifting + Faith + Consecration = Power

The idea is that the amount of authority, gifting, faith and consecration you develop will combine to determine, in large part, the amount of supernatural power you have for ministry. Simple, right?

Authority, gifting, faith and consecration are the four general categories that I think best capture what the Lord has taught us about growing in power. I'll define what I mean by each of them, but first I want to point out a few things about why it's helpful to think along the lines of an equation.

The thing about equations is that they're supposed to equate. The stuff on the left side should equate with the stuff on the right side. If your power requirement (right side) is small—meaning, you're not trying to do anything too daring—then you won't need much authority, gifting, faith or consecration (left side). But if you need more power because, say, you're trying to heal the sick or cast out demons, then you'll need more authority, gifting, faith and consecration. As your power requirements rise, then your level of authority, gifting, faith and consecration must rise to equal it. If one side goes up, the other side must go up.

This presumes what I think is a good thing to keep in mind: some supernatural works seem to require more power than others (it's probably easier to heal hay fever than cancer). Of course, there's no thermometer that tells us exactly how much power we have or need in any given situation. So, the important thing is the overall idea: if we seem to lack the necessary power, then it will help to try to grow in our components of power.

A second, very related point is that equations have variables, meaning that the elements can vary in their amounts. The amount of authority, gifting, faith or consecration you have can rise or fall depending on what you do. The trick—the main thing, really—is to identify and do the things that cause the amounts to go up!

That brings up a third point. You might notice that my power equation has several components being added together. Practically, this means that a lot of one thing can help compensate for a low amount of another. For example, if you're not gifted in healing ministry, but you do have a lot of faith, then your overall power level might still be enough to pull off a given healing. A lot of faith can sometimes make up for a lack of gifting. Or a lot of gifting can make up for a lack of authority. Or some serious consecration can make up for a lack of faith. No single component determines everything.

I stress this point because of some popular misunderstandings. Perhaps the most famous is what's sometimes called "faith healing" or "word of faith" theology. It claims that miracles happen when you really, really believe they will, and that's all there is to it. It's a monovariable explanation. So, if the miracle doesn't happen, you're told that it's always because somebody didn't believe enough. Period.

I think faith has an immense influence on the flow of supernatural power, but it's not the whole story, and assuming that it is can do harm. Imagine a cancer sufferer who fails to see healing, and the "faith healer" says, "Well, you just didn't have enough faith!" That's a devastating thing to say to a discouraged sick person, and it's usually unnecessary. In the Bible, we read how dead people are occasionally brought back to life by Jesus or his followers. How much faith does a dead person have? Not much, I bet. And yet dead people get healed. So, go figure.

OK, you might say, if it's not the faith of the recipient that counts, maybe it's the faith of the minister. But if there were any minister in the Bible who had perfect faith, who would it be? I'd pick Jesus. Yet when Jesus went to his hometown, "he could do no miracles there" because the people "took offense at him," and he was "astonished at their lack of faith" (Mark 6:1-6, my translation). In other words, even Jesus' perfect faith didn't allow him to do all the miracles he wanted!

If it's not the recipient's faith and it's not the minister's faith, maybe it's the combination of the two. And, yes, I think it's true that the amount of faith to do a miracle is the collective faith of everyone present (which is why Jesus sometimes kicked doubters out of the area when he performed certain miracles). But even that's not the whole story. For example, in 2 Kings we read a curious account about Elisha the miracle-working prophet. "Elisha died and was buried," it says. "Now, Moabite raiders used to enter the country every spring. Once while some Israelites were burying a man, they suddenly saw a band of raiders; so they threw the man's body into Elisha's tomb. When the body touched Elisha's bones, the man came to life and stood up on his feet" (2 Kings 13:20-21). So, one dead guy healed another dead guy. Which one of the dead guys do you think had the faith for the healing?

While simplicity is good, overly narrow thinking can cloud the truth and lead to damage.

For my part, I think that most of what the Lord teaches about developing power can be grouped more or less into just the four categories I list. Four is more than one, but it doesn't seem terribly complicated.

So, let's consider the four components in turn and examine how we can grow in each.

Authority

Authority can be defined as our right to wield the power of the Lord. In the kingdom of God, though, it's important to think of rights as *privileges* rather than *entitlements*. Our power privileges increase to the degree we use them as the Lord directs. After all, God always gives us power to do what he tells us to do.

> God always gives us power to do what he tells us to do.

When Jesus first sent out his twelve disciples, he "gave them authority to drive out impure spirits and to heal every disease and sickness." He subsequently commanded, "As you go . . . heal the sick, raise the dead, cleanse those who have leprosy, drive out demons" (Matthew 10:1, 7-8). When his disciples later returned from the mission, they exclaimed, "Lord, even the demons submit to us in your name!" (Luke 10:17). We can speak in the authority of Jesus' name when we are working in obedience to him.

In the Army a private has no command authority. But if a private is called into the supreme general's office and given written orders with the general's signature, the private can then issue commands based on the general's name—provided that the private issues orders in keeping with those given him. The private's authority is based on obedience to the general.

Similarly, our level of authority is determined by our obedience to our leader, Jesus. "If you remain in me and my words remain in you," Jesus says in John 15:7, "ask whatever you wish, and it will be done for you." If you want his "kingdom to come," then let his "will be done" in your life (Matthew 6:10).

In short, obedience to God increases our authority to wield his power.

If you want more authority, seek opportunities for obedience.

It makes sense that God would design things in such a way that those who are most obedient to him would have the most power to do super-

> If you want more authority, seek opportunities for obedience.

natural things, because it helps the world to associate obedience with God's blessings. It also makes sense operationally. Imagine you were an alcoholic and you tried to cast a demon of addiction out of a suffering drug user. If addiction controls you, it's unlikely that a spirit of addiction would feel intimidated by your command, no matter how many times you spoke the name of Jesus. Your disobedience to the Lord would compromise your ability to speak for him.[13]

One of my favorite stories about this sort of thing comes from Acts 19. In Ephesus, "God did extraordinary miracles through Paul," and some non-Christian Jewish priests subsequently tried to duplicate Paul's miracles by merely copying his methods:

> Some Jews who went around driving out evil spirits tried to invoke the name of the Lord Jesus over those who were demon-possessed. They would say, "In the name of the Jesus, whom Paul preaches, I command you to come out." Seven sons of Sceva, a Jewish chief priest, were doing this. One day the evil spirit answered them, "Jesus I know, and Paul I know about, but who are you?" Then the man who had the evil spirit jumped on them and overpowered them all. He gave them such a beating that they ran out of the house naked and bleeding. (Acts 19:13-16)

When the demon realized the priests didn't have a real relationship of obedience with Jesus, he discounted their authority, and then it was all over except for the blood and nudity.

When Jesus spent forty days in the wilderness overcoming temptations, I think he was doing an exercise of obedience to God for the sake of authority. It explains why he returned from the wilderness "in power." Every temptation is an opportunity to choose obedience and grow in authority.

There are a number of passages in which Christ's obedience is connected directly with his power. In Matthew 8:8-9 a centurion tells Jesus to "just say the word, and my servant will be healed," adding, "I myself am a man under authority, with soldiers under me." He knew that since Jesus was under God's authority, he could wield God's authority. So too, when Jesus was criticized for healing a blind man on the sabbath, he responded, "the Son . . . can do only what he sees his Father doing," correlating his authority to heal with his obedience to the Father (John 5:19).

Along similar lines, Jesus sometimes helped along his miracle ministry by creating opportunities for the recipients to obey in the moment, thus increasing the means for God's power to flow in them. For example, ever notice that Jesus often healed people by commanding them to do things? Sometimes the things seemed a little odd. In Mark 2 he commanded a paralyzed man to "stand up, pick up your mat, and walk!" I mean, why bother to mention the mat? In John 9 Jesus went so far as to smear mud in a blind man's eyes and then ordered him to go wash in a pool. Why not just straight-up heal the eyes? Why the theatrics?

I think Jesus was manufacturing opportunities to obey. Active obedience in a situation adds power to the situation. A thing done in obedience is a thing that releases power.

For those of us who want more power for ministry, the application is clear: we get more authority by being more obedient to God, and we lose authority by being disobedient. So, we should look for chances to obey God. This applies to familiar scriptural commands ("preach," "heal," "be generous") as well as specific, personal directions from the Lord. If the Spirit leads you into the wilderness, as he did Jesus, then follow quickly. If the Lord directs you to be a missionary in the Congo, buy the plane ticket.[14] Every command the Lord gives in our lives is an opportunity. When we obey at a high level, we're privileged to wield power at a high level.

We can also look for ways to exercise obedience while in the moment of doing supernatural works. For example, when Peter saw Jesus walking on the stormy sea, he wanted to join in the miracle, so he said, "Lord, . . . tell me to come to you" (Matthew 14:28). Peter instinctively reasoned that he could do the impossible if he were doing it out of obedience to Jesus' word.

I constantly pray for God's direction when I do supernatural ministry, hoping he'll give me a word about a certain healing I should try that day or a prophecy I should give or any specific way to go about ministry. If the Lord bids it specifically, I have that much more authority to pull it off!

On the flip side, when I think about authority and power, my disobedience feels costlier to me. Disobedience to God is always bad, of course, but when I fail to free an eight-year-old suffering from epilepsy, I regret my sin in an added way. My sin doesn't merely affect me; it also affects those who would benefit from the Spirit's power flowing through me better. It makes me crave repentance even more strongly.

It's probably worth mentioning that while disobedience decreases your supernatural power for ministry, it doesn't decrease God's love for you. It's wrong to think that obedience makes God love you and that this in turn causes him to give you power. That's not it at all, because we know God's love for us never varies. We don't obey and minister in order to get God to love us; we do it because God loves us.

Gifting

Most people have some understanding of spiritual gifts. We'll say things such as "she's a gifted preacher" or "he's a gifted musician," recognizing that some people seem specially equipped by God in certain areas. Paul tells the Corinthians, "I don't want you to be ignorant about spiritual gifts," adding, "Everyone receives a manifestation of the Spirit," so everyone should try to embrace and understand them. Different Bible passages list many examples of gifts that God gives supernaturally: prophecy, words of wisdom, healing, discerning of spirits, tongues, interpretation of tongues, helps, teaching, encouragement, giving, leadership, mercy, arts, craftsmanship and others (1 Corinthians 12:1-11; Romans 12:6-8; Exodus 31:1-5). The point isn't to have an exhaustive menu of gifts but to recognize that gifts are plentiful, specific and purposeful.

Maybe this is obvious, but here's the deal with spiritual gifts: where you have a spiritual gift, you will experience more power than where you don't. Spiritual gifts give us a power boost in the specific ministry area they apply to. They're God's way of giving every individual a leg up in some ministry.

It's not necessary that we be gifted in a certain ministry in order to do that ministry, but it helps a lot. For example, most everyone can sing, but if you made everyone at your church sing a solo, you would immediately (and perhaps painfully) discern who had a gift of singing. Teaching is identified as a spiritual gift in Scripture, but does one need to be a gifted teacher to teach something? Of course not, but it's a big advantage. Do you need the gift of healing to heal someone? No, but you'll have an easier time with healings if you do. Do you need the gift of prophecy to hear supernaturally from God? No, in Scripture many people hear from God on occasion, but it's gifted people who seem to be picking up supernatural information all the time. While we can do things that we're not gifted to do, having the right gift increases our capacity to do them—our power to do them. Healing gifts increase power for healing, prophetic gifts for prophesying and so on.

So then the obvious question is, How do we get a certain spiritual gift if we don't already have it? For example, if you wanted to become more powerful in healing people, how would you go about getting the gift of healing?

There are two general answers. One, ask for it. God can bestow new gifting, a process some believers call impartation. I've seen horribly awkward preachers become powerful speakers after simply praying for the gift. I've watched others receive powerful prophetic gifts out of nowhere after earnestly petitioning God. Paul tells the

Corinthians to "eagerly desire the greater gifts," by which he means
to pursue the gifts most useful in caring for the people at hand
(1 Corinthians 14:1). If you need a certain gift to serve well, ask God
to impart it to you. Ask your partners to pray for you too. Gifts can
be imparted from person to person with the blessing of the Holy
Spirit, which is perhaps what Paul was speaking about when he told
Timothy, "Don't neglect your gift, which was given to you with a
prophetic word when the elders laid their hands on you" (1 Timothy
4:14, my translation).[15]

The second way to get a gift is to borrow it. I particularly like this
method because it's relatively lazy. Here's how it works: if you're going
to work in a disease-ridden area and you seem to have no healing gift,
you could spend time petitioning God to give it to you, or you could
grab the guy in your church who already has the gift and bring him
along. Whether you possess the gift or work with someone who pos-
sesses it, your ministry benefits. Teamwork counts.

In fact, teamwork is precisely what Paul was writing about in his
famous essay on spiritual gifts in 1 Corinthians 12: "Everyone is given
a manifestation of the spirit, and all must be used for the common
good. . . . The body is one unit, though it has many parts." We need
each other if we're going to have a complete tool kit for thorough
ministry. By spreading around different spiritual gifts to different
people, God cleverly gives us incentive to reach out to one another—to honor one another and promote unity. The broad distribution of gifts also encourages us to cultivate empowered churches
instead of just relying on empowered individuals.

Accordingly, we need to get good at identifying the array of gifts
in people so we can borrow them when needed. How does one tell if
someone has a given gift? Well, God might reveal it prophetically,
but it's also good to simply try and see. Jesus said that you know a
tree by its fruit. You can tell a gifted musician by listening. You can

tell gifted teachers by the way people learn around them. If you want to identify healers, let people try to heal the sick.

Years ago I felt called to stir up healing ministry in the church, but it seemed to me that I wasn't all that gifted in it. So, I started inviting sick people to my home and, with a bit of bribery, encouraged a group of young people from my church to come and try their hand at healing. You could call it an audition. One young guy, Josh, who had almost no experience in supernatural ministry, quickly racked up a number of healings, so I began dragging him along when I spoke at conferences or seminars. I thoroughly exploited him. It helped a ton. Nowadays, at my church, we're always "auditioning" in some way or another to determine people's gifts.

If you need a gift, go get it—by seeking it yourself or by using what God has given your partners—and you'll have more power.

Gifting is only one ministry factor among others, and it should not necessarily determine what ministry you do; it only determines how you go about doing it. For example, healing still doesn't come easily to me, but I do healing ministry wherever I go, even if I'm working alone, because there always seems to be an abundance of sick people. I compensate for my lack of gifting by having a good amount of faith and by using my gifts of leadership, teaching and prophecy to inspire faith in those around me. I try to work with gifted healers if I can, but sometimes I just have to use what I have. We shouldn't ever refuse to do needed ministry just because we're not gifted at it.

Faith

Believers know that faith can move mountains (Matthew 21:21). The role of faith is mentioned specifically in at least twenty-seven miracle accounts in the Gospels. Nine times Jesus says to a recipient of healing, "Your faith has made you well" or something similar. When the disciples fail at a healing, Jesus indicts them for having so little faith (Matthew 17:19-20). Clearly, more faith means more power.

But faith in what, exactly? We could say we need faith that a given miracle is going to happen, which is true. But when it comes right down to it, I think it's more helpful to have faith about why it's going to happen.

The leper in Mark 1 speaks for generations when he says to Jesus, "If you are willing, you can make me clean." Jesus, "filled with compassion," replies, "I'm willing." We believe that God can do miracles, but either because miracles are so unusual or because we suspect God is displeased with us, we often doubt that he wants to. But Jesus says, "Which of you, if your son asks for bread, will give him a stone? . . . How much more will your Father in heaven give good gifts to those who ask?" (Matthew 7:9-11). Bread is a good gift and so are works of healing, deliverance, revelation or provision. Supernatural ministry is kind and helpful. Of course God is willing to empower you to help the suffering person in front of you.

God's main goal is to encourage us to trust his love, so it makes perfect sense that he would arrange things so that power flows most easily through those who fully trust his compassionate generosity in providing it. So, I'd put it this way: Miracle-working faith believes that God is genuinely eager for the goodness of miracles.

Miracle-working faith believes that God is genuinely eager for the goodness of miracles.

Along those lines it seems to me that the most potent stories of faith are those in which people trust in God's generosity for miracles despite having excuses to believe that God won't allow them. For instance, the hemorrhaging woman in Mark 5 was considered spiritually unclean due to her bleeding. She was not supposed to go out in public. But she defied moral customs, went into the crowd, sneaked up on Jesus and touched him without permission, thinking, *If I just touch his clothes, I'll be healed.* By rights, she should have felt ashamed of her behavior; instead, she was expectant. Jesus suspended an urgent journey to publicly praise her: "Daughter, your faith has healed you!" (vv. 28, 34)

In Matthew 15 Jesus told a Canaanite woman straight-out that he wouldn't minister to her sick daughter because it wasn't yet time for him to focus on the Gentiles. But the resilient woman replied, "Even the dogs eat the crumbs from their master's table." (Paraphrase: "Surely you could spare a little bit of ministry!") Jesus just couldn't resist. "Woman, you have great faith!" he exclaimed. "Your request is granted!" (vv. 26-28). Jesus gets excited when people have a stubborn expectation of God's generosity.

So, the million-dollar question is, What can we do to get more of this sort of faith?

Well, anything that helps us trust that God is generous increases our miracle-working faith. Believers should have an entire lifestyle built around taking risks on God's generosity because that's the best way to grow in trust.

In addition to the life experience we bring to ministry, we should also consider doing things in the moment to help fan faith to flame. Faith is a dynamic thing, and it can fluctuate. Peter walked on water quite well until "he saw the wind and became afraid" (Matthew 14:30, my translation). If you want to increase faith for a given miracle, you'll probably want to stoke and provoke faith in the actual moment of ministry.

First, in the moment of ministry you'll want to stoke your own faith. Coaches tell athletes to focus their minds before the game. Fear should be ignored; confidence embraced. When ministering, Jesus sometimes tells people, "Don't be afraid; just believe!" By exercising some positive willfulness in the moment, we often can encourage ourselves into faith. Before my church's healing teams step into a ministry session, I'll tell them, "Get your faith on!" It's not emotionalism; it's resolve.

Since faith is a collective thing, you should also try to maximize your faith environment when you minister. The amount of faith available to do a miracle is the summation of the faith of everyone present. For example, when a group of friends brought a paralytic to Jesus for healing, Jesus responded based on "their faith," not the paralytic's (Mark 2:5). By making faith collective God wisely ensures that we can never become so fixated on the miracles that we forget our primary mission is to spread faith among people. Community always counts. So, you have to think about the faith in the people around you.

> **The amount of faith available to do a miracle is the summation of the faith of everyone present.**

Sometimes you might manage your faith environment by choosing who is present. In Mark 5, as Jesus prepares to resurrect a dead girl, he allows only his three chief disciples to accompany him into her house. Then, before proceeding, he summarily kicks out a group of mourners who were openly mocking his healing attempt. Why? Because resurrection takes a whole lot of power, and Jesus wanted to have as much faith and as little doubt around him as possible. In a similar way, Peter dismissed onlookers from the room before he raised Dorcas (Acts 9:36-42). Big miracles benefit from a pure faith environment.

But usually the key isn't choosing your participants; it's fueling faith in them. In Acts 14 Paul is preaching on the streets of Lystra, an entirely unreached city. In the crowd is a man crippled since birth. "He listened to Paul as he was speaking. Paul looked directly at him, saw that he had faith to be healed, and called out, 'Stand up on your feet!' At that the man jumped up and began to walk" (vv. 8-10).

Paul knew to look for faith in the crowd, and when he found it he used it immediately. But how did this crippled man, who had never before encountered the gospel, so suddenly develop the faith to be healed? "He listened to Paul." I strongly suspect that Paul, clever fellow, was preaching about Jesus' miracles and perhaps telling stories of how he himself had performed healings in Jesus' name. Paul was seeding the crowd with stories. Testimonies are fantastic fuel for generating faith.

At our church we often begin our ministry events by sharing testimonies about recent healings or deliverances. Sometimes healings happen spontaneously while people are listening. We try to provide every opportunity to believe before we even start the ministry.

> Testimonies are fantastic fuel for generating faith.

In short, faith isn't just something we cling to when times are tough; it's something we should actively cultivate for power. Life experiences can develop faith in us, but so can intentional encouragement and discipline. Every supernatural minister needs to become a good manager and cultivator of faith.

Consecration

Consecration refers to the way we dedicate ourselves to the things of God through specific sacrificial acts. The more of ourselves we set apart exclusively for God's use, the larger our capacity to flow in God's supernatural power.

To get a bead on this idea it might be helpful to think about the contest of kingdoms that Jesus so often described: the kingdom of heaven versus the kingdom of the world. In this constant struggle, the power of heaven flows best through places that the kingdom of heaven has already conquered thoroughly—places in which heaven has gained unimpeded right of way. It's similarly helpful for us to find ways to clear away our worldly activities and fleshly concerns—like blocking off a highway from everyday traffic in order to create space for special cargo to move.

The term *consecration* isn't used as much as it once was, so it might be unfamiliar. The word comes from roots meaning "in sacred condition." It's linked to biblical words such as *holy, anointed, sanctified* and others that suggest being set apart for God. It's actually one of the most common concepts in Scripture. For example, early on God's people were taught to keep the sabbath day holy by cleansing it of earthly work. They were later taught to consecrate various implements for temple worship by cleansing them from common usage. When things were set apart entirely for God, God could then use them with exceptional fullness.

Of course, the ultimate aim of these consecration practices was to teach us to be consecrated people. Paul writes that some vessels are used "for noble purposes and some for ordinary purposes. If a man cleanses himself from the latter, he will be an instrument for noble purposes, consecrated, useful to the Master and prepared for any good work" (2 Timothy 2:20-21, my translation).

But how exactly does a person go about consecrating him- or herself for the things of God?

It typically involves giving up our normally acceptable ties to worldly, fleshly things in order to make space for higher, spiritual ones. When Jesus fasted from food for forty days in the wilderness, it wasn't because there's anything wrong with eating; he did it to subject his appetites to heaven's full control. Heaven subsequently owned the right of way to his stomach and all the fleshly willfulness that went with it.

Whatever the specific act of consecration might be, it must be truly costly, otherwise there's no serious contest and no ground gained. For heaven to gain space in us, the world must lose. As King

David once said, "I cannot make a sacrifice that costs me nothing" (1 Chronicles 21:24, my translation). When we start to feel that we're giving away pieces of ourselves for the sake of Jesus' calling, we're becoming consecrated.

There's logic in that. The relationship between self-sacrifice and the Lord's power makes sense because self-sacrifice is the very nature of love, and God is all about love. Jesus said, "Greater love has no one than this: to lay down one's life for one's friends" (John 15:13). By connecting self-sacrifice and power, God helps ensure that the most powerful ministers will also be the most able to love selflessly.

Scripture often shows us that acts of sacrificial consecration release supernatural power. The best example is Jesus' self-sacrifice on the cross, but there are plenty of others. For instance, in Mark 9:14-29 we see the disciples fail to heal a sick, demonized boy. When Jesus arrives to find the teachers of the law arguing with the disciples about it, he immediately diagnoses a bad faith environment. "You unbelieving generation!" he exclaims. After separating the boy from the problematic crowd, Jesus asks the boy's father, "How long has he been like this?" The man describes the boy's severe, lifelong struggle, so Jesus knows it's a tough case. "Everything is possible for one who believes," Jesus says to stoke the father's faith. But after Jesus cast out the demon and healed the child, the disciples asked him privately, "Why couldn't we cast it out?" In public, Jesus had diagnosed and treated a faith deficit, but in private with his disciples, he addressed the cardinal issue: "This kind"—the really tough kind—"can come out only by prayer and fasting." In other words, any minister who needs an especially great amount of supernatural power had better routinely practice consecrating sacrifices.

> The primary purpose of prayer is not to inform God but to consecrate us.

Consecrating sacrifices can come in a host of forms. Prayer can be a form of consecration, because an hour in prayer is an hour in which you belong to heaven and not the world. Indeed, the primary purpose of prayer is not to inform God but to consecrate us. But it depends on how we pray. Casual prayer might bring peace or help focus our faith, but to be consecrating, prayer must be sacrificial. Think of Jesus bleeding from his forehead while praying in Gethsemane, or Elijah with his head between his knees, in birthing position, as he prayed an end to the drought in Israel (1 Kings 18:41-46). We see Jesus pray through the night before choosing the Twelve, and getting up before dawn to pray in preparation for his day. Regular prayer like that requires a serious contest against the fleshliness within you.

Like prayer, praise and worship of God can be powerfully consecrating, provided they involve a sacrificial devotion that seriously contests the worldliness within you. We're told to worship "in spirit and truth" (John 4:23), which suggests a personal thoroughness. The widow gave her last two mites as an offering, and Jesus celebrated it. The sinful woman lavished a costly alabaster jar of perfume on Jesus (probably sacrificing her dowry and chances for marriage), and he honored it lavishly. King David stripped to his undergarments and danced publicly in praise of the Lord. If we significantly sacrifice our resources or our position in worship, then heaven gains territory in us.

Fasting is a great consecrating exercise because it involves forsaking what is earthly in pursuit of heavenly purpose. Any earthly desire can be an object for fasting: food, sleep, sex and other creature comforts are all suggested by Scripture as appropriate for fasting. We can be creative, as long as we're sacrificially intense. Fasting from chocolate for the forty days of Lent is nice, but, alas, it's not challenging enough to defeat the worldliness within you. Jesus went without any food for forty days; that's challenging in a way that might actually help settle something. (Lots of my friends have done forty-day food fasts, but the three- to ten-day fast is more my typical speed.)

Consecration for power is one of the church's deepest traditions. The first disciples "continued in prayer together" for roughly ten days before being empowered by the Spirit on Pentecost (Acts 1:14). Paul and Barnabas were commissioned for their missionary work during a season of "worship with fasting," and the Antioch church sent them off "after they had fasted and prayed" (Acts 13:2-3). Saint Anthony, father of Christian monasticism, famously spent years praying and fasting in the Egyptian desert, and when he returned to civilization, he performed such great and plentiful miracles that Roman persecutors were afraid to touch him. The great American revivalist Charles Finney moved in such power that sometimes people would start sobbing in repentance as soon as he walked into the room. He said that when his power waned he "would then set apart a day for private fasting and prayer" and then "the power would return upon me with all its freshness."[16] Consecration and power have always gone together.

A famous Christian psychologist once told me that "traditions of self-mortification," such as fasting and severe prayer, "are emotionally unhealthy." But I think he was confused about motivations. If you pursue such sacrifices for the sake of worthiness, then you misunderstand grace. But if you pursue them for consecration—to prepare yourself for power—then you've understood something about partnering with God for kingdom work. What you sacrifice to heaven, God gives back to you with power. Whatever you dedicate sacrificially to God, he makes wondrous for you.

Power Relationships

Anyone who gets involved with supernatural ministries will be asked an array of questions having to do with inconsistent or disappointing results. Usually the best way to answer these questions is to think about them in light of how we grow in God's supernatural power.

Why don't miracles always happen when you pray for them? If you fail to get a miracle, does that mean it wasn't God's will to grant it? Well, if the miracle doesn't happen, it might be because God has forbidden it, but it's far more likely that you just haven't developed enough power yet. God works with us, so we might just have more work to do on our end.

Why do some people seem to get more results from, say, praying for healing than other people do? Why don't they always get good results? God's power is unchanging, but people's level of empowerment can vary a great deal according to their recent investments in things like authority, gifting, faith and consecrating self-sacrifice.

Do you need to be specially gifted by God to heal the sick or to hear directly from God? No, particular gifts are never necessary, but they are one of the things that really help boost our ministry power. Spiritual giftedness shouldn't be seen as a limiting factor, but gifts should definitely be identified and cultivated.

If you pray for a person to get healed or delivered, and it doesn't work, what should you do then? You should be sensitive to the person's disappointment and as supportive as can be, but if at all possible you should also go get more power and try again. The key to supernatural ministry is to develop in power. It's helpful if everybody involved understands this so that we're free to respond to people's disappointments with repeated and increased efforts. It's good if everyone has some idea of how to work for supernatural breakthrough.

A friend recently asked me a slightly subtler question: Is it more important to pursue supernatural power for ministry or to simply pursue God and let the power flow as a byproduct? He was concerned that being too ministry-minded might compromise his intimacy with the Lord. But, to reiterate an earlier point, God has worked it out so that all the things that develop supernatural power in us are also things that draw us closer to him.

....

God has worked it out so that all the things that develop supernatural power in us are also things that draw us closer to him.

....

Submitting to God's authority increases our power, but it also tightens our walk of obedience with him. The use of spiritual gifts boosts power, but it also increases our awareness of God's grace in us and encourages us to work together in unity with our brothers and sisters. Increased faith brings power, but faith is also the very bedrock of our relationship with God. Consecration amplifies power, but it also exercises our devotion to heaven and freedom from the world. It's a package deal. Working for spiritual muscle will also get us a healthier spiritual heart.

Each Step

I met my friend David Bunker several years back when he shuffled into a healing seminar I was leading at a conference in the San Francisco area. He was a mess. He had suffered terribly for decades with polio and a condition called peripheral nerve atrophy. Some of the bones in his legs and feet didn't fit together correctly. His muscles were atrophied and so severely shortened in places that his joints could not extend. His nerve problems left him with only partial sensation in his extremities, and he couldn't properly control all the muscles in his legs. He had had fourteen surgeries to help alleviate some of his painful symptoms, and he had suffered with a number of illnesses resulting from his weakened immune system. He wore cumbersome leg braces and had to use canes or crutches to walk. He also wore neoprene wraps on both legs for muscle support and help against poor blood circulation. He couldn't stand or even sit without pain.

And what's more, David wasn't sure he was comfortable being at a supernatural healing seminar. Some friends had forced him to come. But toward the end of the brief seminar, when I called for the sick or injured to move into the aisles for ministry, he did.

I spoke a blessing of healing over the crowd, and though I didn't walk over to David right away, I could see that the Spirit's power was moving in him. For one thing, the people around him were getting excited. He was standing by propping himself on a cane in front of him, but as he leaned there, his legs were shaking in an odd way. His knees were flexing back and forth. His face was flushed and he was sweating noticeably. When I managed to get to him, I gently touched him in his mid-section—which he would later tell me felt like a "painless punch." Then things started to accelerate.

David wore special shoes to cope with his misaligned foot bones and toes, which were permanently curled under the ball of his foot. As we watched, we could see the tops of his shoes bulge and recede as the bones seemed to be moving around. We could also hear popping noises from the joints and bones in his legs.

"It feels like my bones are moving around!" he said.

"Cool," I answered.

He shot me quite a look and said, "That's the first time anyone has ever used the word *cool* with respect to me"—as if that were the most amazing thing happening to him at that moment.

David's right leg started to "dance" involuntarily. His foot bounced a staccato rhythm on the floor. At the same time, he said, his body "relaxed." His muscles eased and he stood straight, which was a new thing for him. Soon the leg twitches subsided.

"Well, let's see you walk," I said. "But lose the cane."

Without hesitation, he passed the cane to a friend and set off on a leisurely stroll around the room, to cheers from his friends.

"OK, showoff, now let's see you walk backwards," I dared him.

He handled it perfectly, without a hint of imbalance or unsteadiness in his gait. Somebody suggested he take off the braces, but he wasn't so sure, yet.

"Well, I'll tell you what," I said, checking my watch, "our time in this hall is up. Why don't you walk back to your hotel room and test things as you go?"

As David was exiting, I felt a nudge from the Lord and called out, "You'll get stronger with each step you take. And your toes will straighten out."

As David walked to his room, he noticed that his braces seemed to have gotten too big—they were "floating" on his legs, he later reported. In the room he took off the braces and walked around without stumbling. He noticed that his left calf muscle, formerly atrophied from disuse, had grown fuller. After more experimenting, he turned in for a good night's sleep, but during the night he woke often and felt surges of power course through his legs and feet. This continued throughout the next day as he walked without his usual supports. He was pain-free for the first time in memory.

At first David thought he should continue to wear the braces for a while, but they would suddenly become loose as his bones seemed to shift around. "It's as if my bones were searching for the proper alignment," he said. And so it went as he figured out, quite literally, how to walk in healing.

A year later, I saw David at the same annual conference. He strode toward me confidently, stopped and opened his arms wide to show me his new form. No one would have thought he had ever suffered with polio or nerve disease. No canes, no braces, no pain.

"Jordan," he said grandly, "I'm even doing yard work!"

He told me a funny story about his doctor looking at the new x-rays taken after the healing session. "Um, something has changed here," the doctor said. David shared his testimony with him. "Well, what can I say?" concluded the doc, "Something happened."

That evening, I was scheduled to do another healing seminar, and David was assigned to be my introducer. He walked up to the microphone.

"The first time I came to a healing seminar, I was wearing these," he said, lifting up his old leg braces, which he then dropped noisily on the podium. "Now I'm not. Welcome to the seminar."

As introductions go, it was definitely cool.

The Ministry of Healing

One of the fascinating things about studying healing ministry in Scripture is the wonderfully diverse way the many stories of healing unfold. Peter's mother-in-law was healed as soon as Jesus took her hand, but the ten lepers didn't experience their healing until after Jesus had sent them away. Jesus healed a servant's ear by touching it, but the hemorrhaging woman was healed when she sneaked up on Jesus and touched him. Jairus's daughter was resurrected from death immediately when Jesus called her, but the blind man in Bethsaida needed Jesus to touch him twice before he saw clearly. Jesus ordered a man to stretch out his withered hand, and the man was healed as he tried the impossible, but the centurion's servant was healed over a considerable distance just by Jesus' word. The paralytic lowered down to Jesus through a roof was first forgiven of his sins and then healed, but when Jesus healed the man born blind, he assured his disciples that sin played no part in the affliction. Jesus first delivered the hunched-back woman from a demonic spirit of infirmity and then touched her spine to heal it, but the Canaanite girl wasn't even present when Jesus delivered and healed her through a proclamation to her mother. Jesus distributed healings through touch, commands and declarations. Sometimes he applied saliva, sometimes mud. Sometimes just touching his cloak was enough.

This emphasizes what should probably already be clear: healing ministry is less about how we do a healing and more about how much power we have when we do it. It's not about the technique used; it's about the power we have in God. It isn't about having ministers who know how to pray for the sick; it's about having ministers who are steeped in the obedience, faith, gifting and consecration that lead to spiritual power. If your healing ministry is going poorly, it's probably not because you're executing healings incorrectly; it's probably just that you need to develop more power.

That said, the way we go about a given healing can sometimes be important in that it can increase the amount of power we have in the moment. By being aware of the things that increase the flow of power, we can sometimes adjust methods to serve best in a given situation. We can do a little on-the-spot empowerment.

For instance, when Jesus said to the paralytic, "Be encouraged, son, your sins are forgiven," I imagine the declaration of forgiveness probably helped the poor, broken-down man to have faith that God would bless him. Faith increases the flow of God's power, so Jesus' clever shepherding probably made the healing easier.

Similarly, when Jesus put mud in the blind beggar's eyes and sent him away to wash in the pool, he required this man who was used to being led about passively to actively obey on his own, which probably increased Christ's authority in him.

There's no right or wrong way to go about healing someone, but there may be ways to cultivate a little extra faith or obedience in the moment, or to leverage certain spiritual gifts that are available around us. As preachers tune their approach based on their listeners, healers can tune their approach based on the people and situations involved.

So in this chapter we'll talk about doing what we can to boost healing power during the healing itself. I'll start by talking about God's attitude toward sickness, since that's foundational to our approach. Then I'll offer a simple healing model and suggest some power-boosting ways to both engage the sick and apply a healing. I'll also discuss what I half-humorously call the thermodynamics of healing, which has to do with how healing power often flows from person to person, and how that sometimes requires time and persistence. I'll add a quick note on sickness and demons (though the full discussion on deliverance ministry will come later). I then want to offer some advice for navigating the emotional challenges of healing ministry, because a little sensitivity to people can go a long way toward producing good fruit. I'll end the chapter with a couple tips for getting started in healing ministry.

God's Attitude

Can we be confident that God wants us to try to heal the suffering person standing in front of us? Actually yes, we should be very confident—bold even. It's theoretically possible that God might refuse to allow a given healing for some reason, but in the kingdom of God, healing is the default position.

> In the kingdom of God, healing is the default position.

Unfortunately, believers can get exceptionally complicated in how they think about God's will for healing. If a person comes to us with life questions, we don't doubt that God wants us to preach the good news to him or her. If we walk into a desperately poor village, we don't doubt that God wants us to feed the hungry. If we were to see a demon manifest in a person, we wouldn't doubt that God wants the demon gone. But for some strange reason when we encounter sickness in a person, some of us worry about whether God wants the sickness healed or if it's God's timing for the healing.

We'd never discourage a sick friend from visiting a doctor, but some of us are wary of presuming on God for a supernatural healing. You'll often hear believers pray, "Lord, if it be thy will . . ." when addressing sickness. And some teachers go so far as to insist that we shouldn't try a healing unless God gives us a specific order to do it. Pointing out that Jesus didn't heal everyone in every village, they infer that he probably just healed the few whom the Father specifically ordered him to heal.

I think this sort of thinking is awfully unhelpful. Sure, Jesus sometimes left places without healing every sickness there, but that doesn't mean that it isn't God's desire that all be healed. In truth, Jesus' healing ministry was fantastically open and generous. We're told that Jesus could only heal "a few sick people" in his hometown because the townsfolk lacked faith and mocked him (Mark 6:1-6). Jesus' miracle working there was hampered by their lack of faith, not by God's permission. Other times, we're told, Jesus couldn't stop to minister to everyone because he had other urgent things to do (Mark 1:32-39). He was just one guy, after all.

Far more instructive for our purposes are the accounts of when Jesus did heal every sick person present. In Matthew 8 many people came to Jesus in the evening, and he "healed all the sick." In Matthew 12 Jesus tried to withdraw to an isolated place, but "many followed him and he healed all their sick." In Matthew 14:36 "many begged him to let the sick just touch the edge of his cloak, and all who touched it were healed." In Luke 4:40 "the people brought to Jesus all who had various kinds of sicknesses, and laying his hands on each one, he healed them." And the list goes on.

In the same vein, when the disciples failed in their attempt to deliver and heal the boy suffering with seizures (Matthew 17:14-21; Mark 9:14-29), Jesus didn't say that God had disallowed it. Instead, he said the problem was their lack of faith and spiritual preparation. Jesus proceeded to heal the boy, suggesting that God had been willing all along.

Another instructive passage comes in Mark 5, where the hemorrhaging woman sneaks up behind Jesus in a crowd, touches his garment and is immediately healed. Jesus stops and asks repeatedly, "Who touched me?" Obviously, he didn't have a specific command from the Father to heal this woman. In fact, he had no idea she was there.

Amazingly, even when Jesus did have a mind to be cautious about God's will for dispensing healing, it didn't necessarily get in the way of healing. In Matthew 15, Jesus initially refuses to heal the Canaanite woman's daughter because, as he explained, it was precisely not God's plan that he minister to the Gentiles yet. However, when the woman overwhelms Jesus with her show of faith, he excitedly relents, "and her daughter was healed at that moment" (v. 28). The Father's will is all about fostering faith in people, and so despite his sense that his mission was meant first for the people of Israel, Jesus honored the faith he found.

This is what healing ministers need to know: God's will is that his followers should have power over sickness. To respect God's will means to seek and apply that power. Is it possible that sometimes God doesn't want a given person to be healed at a given time? Sure, given God's creative and mysterious ways, it's possible. For instance, you could argue that God would not have allowed successful healing ministry for Job because the Lord had such purpose in his physical suffering. But clearly, in general, God's healing agenda is pretty wide open.

Jesus taught us to pray that God's "kingdom come on earth as it is in heaven." No one is lost in heaven, so when kingdom people encounter darkness, they preach the truth. There's no poverty in heaven, so when kingdom people encounter poverty, they try to bring justice. There's no oppression in heaven, so when we encounter the demonized and downtrodden, we try to bring deliverance. And there's no sickness in heaven, so when we encounter sickness, we try to bring healing. It's not complicated.

If we were to encounter a little boy dying of infection, and we had a vial of penicillin, we would offer it without a second thought because it would be the compassionate and godly thing to do. Supernatural healing is also compassionate and godly, so we should offer it freely.

If Jesus wanted us to be careful about dispensing healing, he probably would have mentioned it somewhere amid his dozens of healing episodes and related teachings. Instead, his instructions on healing ministry come across like broad standing orders. Four out of the five times that Jesus exhorts his disciples to declare the kingdom message, he also commands them to heal the sick. When John the Baptist questions Jesus' identity, Jesus tells his messengers,

> Go back and report to John what you hear and see: The blind receive sight, the lame walk, those who have leprosy are cleansed, the deaf hear, the dead are raised, and the good news is proclaimed to the poor. (Matthew 11:4-5)

It's as if all these things, taken together, are evidence of Christ's kingdom. On Jesus' instruction the disciples "went out and preached that people should repent. They drove out many demons and anointed many sick people with oil and healed them" (Mark 6:12-13). Jesus encourages us to administer the kingdom in all ways at once.

....

Four out of the five times that Jesus exhorts his disciples to declare the kingdom message, he also commands them to heal the sick.

....

Of course, our healing ministry might not work perfectly, but then, our preaching ministry doesn't either. We shouldn't abandon either one just because it's difficult.

I'm often asked, doesn't God sometimes use sicknesses to develop character in people? God uses many different sorts of challenges to develop us, but that doesn't mean he doesn't want us to overcome them. Heal the sickness if you can; God can come up with new challenges for us if necessary.

Doesn't sickness sometimes come from sin in people's lives, and don't people need to get the sin ironed out before healing can happen? I guess you could argue that all sickness is the result of humankind's fall, and certainly some sicknesses result from specific sin (for example, if you abuse drugs, your body gets hurt). But when the disciples asked Jesus if the man was born blind due to his sin or his parents' sin, Jesus said, "Neither this man nor his parents sinned, but this happened so that the works of God might be displayed in him" (John 9:1-3). Jesus sometimes declared blanket forgiveness for people before healing them, but he never asked anyone to repent of sins before healing. In any case, an undeserving person who experiences God's merciful healing might well be motivated to repent later out of thankfulness.

> In healing, as in all ministry, we help ourselves by being sensitive, but not by being timid.

But what if it's just the person's time to die? Well, everyone dies, so presumably there comes a time for every individual when God disallows healing. But how can you tell when that time has come? A minister needs to be sensitive at the side of every deathbed (we'll talk about this later), but I try to bring the kingdom's power to everyone at every time. As I sometimes say to my very elderly brothers and sisters, "God can take you home if he wants to, but I'm going to try to see that you die healthy."

In healing, as in all ministry, we help ourselves by being sensitive, but not by being timid. We might not be sure of the specific will of God in every instance, or be certain of success in every healing, but we can be quite sure of our calling to bring the kingdom—and its healing—to whomever we meet. "And these signs will accompany those who believe:... they will place their hands on sick people, and they will get well" (Mark 16:17-18). That's a wide-open statement.

The Model (Such as It Is)

Technique is not the key to healing; having the supernatural power of the Lord is the key. But we have to go about healing in some fashion, and we'll probably benefit from having a basic approach from which to build and adjust as opportunities for power present themselves.

So, here's a model.

1. Locate a sick person.

2. Place a hand on the person's shoulder and say, "In the name of Jesus, be healed."

That's pretty much it.

If you want to get fancier, you might try variations: "In the name of Jesus, leg, be healed" (this one works especially well for leg problems). "In the name of Jesus, fever, be broken" (I often use this one for, you know, fevers). "In Jesus' name, stomach, get better" (recommended for digestive issues).

In other words, you don't need much training to figure it out. Try this model once or twice, and you will have mastered it completely. Congratulations.

But while you can master the necessities of the model in just a few minutes, there are endless ways you can build into and through it. That's where the payoffs are. So, with this basic model as a general guide, I like to encourage healing ministers to think in terms of three steps for healing ministry: preparing, engaging and applying. Preparing is the big one, of course. You can't do much of anything unless you've grown in the Spirit's power. If you have, then it's just a matter of maximizing it through the way you engage the sick and apply the healing. Your preparation with respect to authority, faith, gifting and consecration will help you bring a lot of power to every healing opportunity.

But we've already talked a lot about preparing. So here we'll focus on engaging and applying.

Engage

You'll have to engage the sick person in some way, and it's wise to make the most of it. The way we engage people will help the flow of God's power if it increases their faith or provokes some sort of bold obedience that strengthens Christ's authority in them. The trick is to not demand faith or obedience from people but to motivate it. We're not looking for empty acquiescence but for spiritual investment from them.

There are numerous instances of Jesus and his apostles healing people without much engagement: sometimes people would merely touch them and be healed; sometimes Jesus and the apostles healed at a distance; sometimes the crowds were such that one imagines there wasn't much time or space for conversation. But often the record gives us stories of masterful interactions that paved the way for power to flow.

I think again of Jesus' interaction with the father of the mute boy with terrible seizures (Mark 9:14-29). The disciples had tried but failed to heal the boy, which probably unleashed a wave of faith-numbing disappointment. When Jesus shows up, he separates the boy from the dubious crowd (thus managing the faith environment) and then asks the father, "How long has he been like this?" The father answers, "From childhood! But if you can do anything, please help!"

Jesus says, "Anything is possible for him who believes." Without confronting or manipulating, Jesus is provoking the man's faith.

The man responds with one of the great prayers of Scripture: "I do believe; help me overcome my unbelief!" (v. 24). He had started with an uncertain petition ("If you can . . . help!") but has now switched to humble participation ("I believe, just help me believe more!"). This bit of added faith is enough for Jesus, and he immediately heals the child.

Sometimes, we can generate a little faith and authority just by making an interaction very personal. When a crippled beggar asked Peter and John for money, the disciples "looked directly at him," and Peter said, "Look at us!" (Acts 3:4). They moved from the dull routine of begging to the intense experience of people locking eyes. This surely stirred the man's expectation, and when Peter pulled him to his feet, he was healed.

Sometimes, an empowering interaction can be even simpler. A huge crowd followed Jesus near Jericho, and when Bartimaeus the blind man heard Jesus was near, he began shouting, "Son of David, have mercy on me!" (Mark 10:46-52). "Many rebuked him" for being bothersome, which tells you just how long and loud the guy shouted. Eventually, Jesus called for him and asked, "What do you want me to do for you?"

Obviously, Jesus didn't really need to ask this question. Bartimaeus's blindness was plain enough, and everyone had already heard his pleas. But Jesus saw that Bartimaeus had enough stubborn faith to defy the crowd's rebukes, so he took a moment to fan that faith right before doing the miracle. Jesus' question—"What do you want me to do?"—prompted what amounted to a declaration of faith: "Teacher, I want to see!"

At our healing services, I find that a simple "What do you want today?" will often provoke individuals to overcome their nervousness and activate the faith that brought them to the service in the first place.

Different spiritual gifts can also be used to shape engagements in an empowering way. For instance, I love to use prophecy to set up healings at our church services. When it comes time for healing ministry, one of our prophetic ministers might say to the crowd, "I think the Lord is telling me that there's a woman here with a swollen thyroid gland. It was just diagnosed this week, and the Lord wants us to heal it. Is there someone here with that condition?" Almost always, someone will raise a hand in response, and we'll start by ministering to the person. That person usually has greater faith because the Lord has singled him or her out with a revelation, and the crowd gains faith from watching it all.

Teaching is another spiritual gift I like to leverage when engaging people. I'm a decent teacher, which means that when I teach, people often "get it." I've found that if I take just five minutes to teach something about grace or love before a healing session, then people have an easier time trusting God's goodness during the course of the healing ministry. Jesus often coupled healing ministry with teaching, and I suspect his grace-filled teachings made the healing easier.

In any case, the gift of healing is not the only gift that's useful in healing ministry. Anything that builds faith or sparks bold obedience is great, and we should use whatever tools we have.

> The gift of healing is not the only gift that's useful in healing ministry.

On the flip side, when engaging the sick, we'll want to avoid things that dampen faith or complicate obedience. For example, although it's sometimes convenient to have the person explain his or her health condition to you, it can be very unhelpful to discuss the whole sordid medical history. Speaking at length about frustration and pain doesn't necessarily put a person in an expectant frame of mind. Sometimes, the burden of sickness being what it is, people will seek sympathy at the expense of faith, and you'll want to refocus the interaction. You'll definitely want to avoid anything that might make a sick person feel judged. People burdened by sickness often feel shameful about it. We need to help them overcome unbelief, not point a finger at it.

Engaging the sick is not rocket science. Common sense goes a long way. You should avoid making sweeping guarantees of healing because (1) you're probably not that powerful yet, and (2) it can sometimes intimidate folks who have been struggling. But it's great to share stories about when you've seen people healed of conditions similar to the ones at hand. Testimonies build faith far better than pretentious guarantees. It helps to be encouraging and to express your confidence in God's heart. In general, sickness can make people feel alone and adrift, so a little old-fashioned love and affection can really help.

Apply

After engaging people, you apply the power to heal them. To apply power means to conduct, discharge or direct the healing. It's how we trigger the healing.

Earlier, I suggested you might apply power to a sick person by laying on a hand and saying something like, "In the name of Jesus, be healed!" This works just fine, but it's only one example of the principle.

I have a dog that I sort of rescued from a bad situation, and when I first got her, she was completely untrained and frequently violent. But through a lot of effort over time I've gained power over her. To exercise that power, I often use verbal commands, but sometimes I just snap my fingers, touch her haunches, tug her leash or even just stare at her with a certain look. She respects them all because she respects me. I'm free to use whatever trigger is most convenient.

A similar dynamic takes place when executing power over

sickness. If you have the power, then you just need to do something to exert it. The trigger can be a command, a declaration, a firm touch or an application of anointing oil—any means of taking charge of the situation will do. There are no rules about how to apply healing.

However, sometimes the way you choose to apply power can be extra helpful in getting the sick person to receive it in faith or obedience. In this you can think of application as an extension of engagement. In fact, the things that you do to provoke faith or authority in the person might suggest a way of exercising that faith or authority.

For example, the crippled man at the pool of Bethesda had been invalid for thirty-eight years and had become terribly discouraged (John 5:1-9). The water at this pool was reputed to be stirred every so often by an angel, at which point it became healing water. True believers gathered there to be healed, but the man had been there a long time, and Jesus sensed he had given up. So, he engages the man provocatively: "Do you want to get well?" The man complains, "I have no one to help me into the pool when the water is stirred. While I am trying to get in, someone else goes down ahead of me" (v. 7). The man felt like a victim. So, Jesus applies healing with the sort of bold command that would snap him out of his victim mentality: "Get up! Pick up your mat and walk." It's as if Jesus were saying, "Be powerful, brother!" The man acts, and he's healed instantly.

I don't want to overanalyze things, but I sometimes like to think in terms of antidotes when choosing a means of applying healing. For instance, if the sick person seems beaten down by discouragement, I might use a direct healing command to provoke her to respond with courage. If the person's sickness seems to make him feel dirty or untouchable, I'll definitely use touch (as Jesus did with lepers).

Other times, I just think about making the most of advantages I see. If the person seems full of faith, I might use declarations over them. I'll declare, "You're healed," instead of saying, "Be healed." Jesus often did exactly this when he said something like, "Go, your faith has healed you." Such declarations encourage people to rest in the faith they have rather than to worry about needing more faith. Jesus also used declarations when healing people who weren't present (the centurion's servant, the Canaanite woman's daughter) because such declarations were the best way to make the most of the faith of the people who were present (the centurion, the mother). He couldn't say, "Be healed" to someone who wasn't there, but he could leverage the faith at hand by declaring, "The person you love is healed!"

Still other times, the person's physical condition might suggest the use of certain triggers. When Jesus healed deaf people, he touched their ears instead of just speaking commands—for obvious reasons.

In any event, whether you've laid hands on someone, given a command, declared healing or used some combination, you'll want the person to exercise the healing right away whenever possible. If the person is crippled, have him try to walk. If the person is deaf, test her hearing. If the healing can be tested immediately, then test it. And do it confidently. Telling people to test the healing is often part of applying it. It's like giving them permission to be healed. More practically, it's just the best way to determine if the healing worked.

Frequently, a healing application will unfold with manifestations. For example, the sick person might feel power in the form of heat or "electricity" in his or her body

> Telling people to test the healing is often part of applying it. It's like giving them permission to be healed.

parts, or affected muscles will twitch, or affected limbs will quiver involuntarily. Occasionally, affected parts will hurt suddenly as, say, muscles grow or twisted joints straighten. The sensations are unimportant in themselves, but they indicate that changes are happening supernaturally. So, when such sensations occur, work with them.

Use them to keep the faith and obedience flowing: "Hey, that's a great sign! Let's keep going!" Sensations don't always happen, but when they do, they give us something extra to use.

Most of the time it's good to choose a method of applying healing that empowers the recipient best, but sometimes it's important to choose a method that empowers you best. For example, if God specifically tells you to use a declaration or a touch, then you should definitely obey that guidance because, among other reasons, your obedience will increase your authority. Or if you feel a manifestation of healing power or heat in your hands, then, by all means, lay those hands on people. If you're a gifted prophet or leader, then spoken declarations might be comfortable for you and help you to flow in faith. Techniques are entirely negotiable, so it's fine to simply pick what you like best. The only caveat is that you must not avoid any technique out of fear. If you're too timid to speak a healing word, I'd encourage you to speak out anyway, because faith flows best when fear is conquered.

With a basic model in your head, you're in a good position to feel your way through it, and that's what you should do, because healing ministry isn't a formulaic mechanism; it's an empowered interaction between people.

The Thermodynamics of Healing

Just as healing methods can vary, the way healing unfolds will look different in different cases. For example, sometimes persons receiving healing have sensations of heat or electric tingling in their bodies, but just as often there will be no special sensations. A much more important variation has to do with time. Some healings will happen immediately, but others will take a while. We need to be ready for this.

Healing ministry has a sort of thermodynamic quality in that it involves the flow of power. Thermodynamics is the physical science given to the study of the way heat flows through objects. When you minister healing to people, you're essentially releasing into them the current of supernatural power the Lord has given you.

Sometimes this thermodynamic quality is more obvious than others. For instance, just like heat, supernatural power can flow into and through various materials. In Mark 5 the woman is healed by the charge of power carried in Jesus' cloak. In Acts 19 Paul touched a number of handkerchiefs and aprons that were then passed around the city, and everyone who touched the items was healed or delivered. When a powerful person handles an object, the object can be infused with power, and others can then receive power via the object. The way some churches use anointing oil or healing cloths is based on this principle.

Like anything that flows from one place to another, healing power can take a little time to get where it's going. The way power moves and saturates is dynamic—it varies depending on different things. And so the time it takes can also vary. Practically, this means that healing ministers sometimes need to be patient and stick with it.

In Mark 8 Jesus sets about healing a blind man. He spits on the man's eyes and lays his hands on him. "Do you see anything?" Jesus asks. "I see trees that look like men walking," says the blind man. In other words, the man had started to see a little, but the images were still blurry. So, Jesus again puts his hands over the man's eyes to apply a bit more power, a bit more flow. After the second effort, the man sees perfectly. Sometimes even Jesus had to take multiple whacks. And if Jesus himself had to try twice, we might need to give it twenty tries.

Accordingly, it's not uncommon to see partial healings in people, meaning that only part of the affliction is healed during the first ministry session. A person's congestive heart failure might be healed, but high blood pressure may persist. Or a deaf person's hearing might improve but not be perfect.

In cases of partial or incremental healing, I'll repeat my attempts for full healing as long as I have time to try. I might lay hands on a person three or four times in one healing service. Sometimes the person gets a bit better each time. Sometimes I have to send the person away with a partial healing and promise to try again later. Sometimes the healing gradually progresses through the night or over a few days. In serious cases my partners and I might minister to someone for many hours or around the clock or return day after day as we try to get the power to flow further. In between sessions we'll do things to increase our authority, faith and consecration, or recruit gifted people to help. I've seen a crippled man get healed over a couple of days, and a woman with multiple sclerosis regain use of her limbs over the course of months.

The need for repetition shouldn't be a deterrent. Healing ministry is about the flow of power, and sometimes it's about persisting in the things that improve it. We prepare, engage and apply, and then sometimes we reprepare, reengage and reapply. This might just be part of the process, and if it is, it will create unique opportunities for exercising faith and love.

Sickness and Demons

Occasionally, as we're trying to heal someone, we'll discover that the affliction is actually being caused by the presence of a demon in the person's body.

Yeah, it's weird, but it happens.

We'll talk in a later chapter about how to recognize demons and drive them out. But for now it's worth stressing that demonic encounters in healing ministry shouldn't surprise us. If evil spirits exist, they're surely capable of manipulating physical bodies (think of Satan whisking Jesus up to a "high place" during his temptation in the wilderness), and if they can manipulate physical bodies, it's reasonable to think they can affect the health of bodies.

Jesus and his disciples encountered a number of sickness-causing demons. For example, the sick boy brought by his father had what today we would call a neurological affliction (Matthew 17:14-21; Mark 9:14-29). He had dramatic seizures and had lost his ability to speak. But everyone there recognized the presence of a demon, and when Jesus finally cast it out, the boy was completely healed.

The hunched-back woman that Jesus encounters in Luke 13 suffered from what we could call severe scoliosis—a twisted spine. But we're told that her condition was caused by a "spirit of infirmity." Accordingly, Jesus first declares her freedom (effectively dismissing the demon) and then proceeds to lay on hands to heal the spine.

I once experienced something similar when ministering to a young woman in Boston. She suffered from a liver problem that made it increasingly difficult for her to digest necessary nutrients. During the healing session I sensed prophetically that the disease might be linked to the presence of an evil spirit, and I started to ask her a few questions to investigate. Suddenly, I felt the power of the Lord surge into my body with an accompanying sense of God's indignation. I immediately commanded, "Demon of shame, let go of her right now!" She instantly felt a change in her body, and simply said, "It's gone." Her liver condition reversed and has never bothered her again.

Some famous healers have claimed that every sickness is caused by demons, but the Gospels plainly treat sickness and demonization as two different things, and the large majority of recorded healing episodes make no mention of casting out demons of infirmity. However, it's fair to say that healing ministry will often involve deliverance, and we should be ready for it.

> Healing ministry will often involve deliverance, and we should be ready for it.

Happily the power to cast out demons is basically the same as the power to heal the sick. As we develop in power for the one, we're helping ourselves with the other. If you bump into a demon when trying to heal someone, the magnitude of your task hasn't really changed all that much. You will have to handle the demon, but that's not necessarily any more challenging than curing the disease.

Pastoring the Sick

Whenever sick people seek healing, they're risking disappointment. This is true whether they work with a doctor or a supernatural minister. But failures in supernatural ministry can especially tempt people to draw inappropriate conclusions about God's will or God's approval. If the assumption is that God heals, but the person doesn't get healed, then the person might become bitter toward God or feel rejected by him, and that's a nasty business we want to avoid.

The solution, of course, is to understand that God partners with us to get healings done, so failures are the product of our imperfections, not God's. If people understand that it's our role and responsibility to develop in God's power for ministry, they'll be far less likely to just bitterly blame God or to feel rejected by him.

But there's a pastoral art to getting people to understand well. It's not necessary for people to understand all the specifics of authority, gifting, faith or consecration for power, but the way we talk about healing ministry can help.

For example, instead of saying things like, "Let's see if the Lord will heal tonight," you can say things like, "Let's see if we can move in the Lord's power tonight." If someone asks, "Why didn't the Lord heal me?" you can say, "The problem is that the Lord's power flows through me, and I'm an imperfect minister." If people understand that it has to do with the flow of power, they'll also understand that healing can take repeated efforts. It helps them work with you.

Unfortunately, if people know that they play a role in their own healing, there's a danger they'll just fall into unhelpful self-recrimination: "I can't get healed because I'm such a loser!" Jesus taught us to avoid the blame game entirely, but some people have a hard time with grace and mercy.

So, in practice, I find that it's best for me to assume all the responsibility for failures myself. Really, a failure might be as much about the person's imperfect receiving as my imperfect power, but, as a shepherd, we can't blame sheep for acting like sheep sometimes. I try to motivate sick people to help me with their faith or obedience, but I won't allow anyone to blame themselves if they don't. My attitude is "We need to work with God to bring healing, and if we fail, please forgive me. I'll keep trying." Once people know that I'm comfortable with accepting the blame, they typically stop worrying about assessing blame, and that's what Jesus would want.

Similarly, people often react to sickness by wondering if the Lord is using it to teach them lessons. This is dangerous because it might convince them that the Lord requires them to be sick, which in turn might discourage them from seeking or expecting healing. Really, even if the Lord sends a certain challenge, there's still almost certainly profit in battling to overcome it. The lessons are usually in the battle. Indeed, if anything, Jesus suggests that sickness exists so that we might heal it (John 9:3).

So, here's my tip: Instead of focusing on what God is teaching through the sickness, focus on what God is teaching through the pursuit of healing. Instead of "sickness teaches us patience," move toward "healing teaches us persistence." Instead of "sickness teaches us to surrender to God," move toward "healing teaches us to follow the Lord."

Finally, the conventional wisdom is that it's healthy for people to accept incurable conditions so that they can learn to live with them or die peacefully from them. There's definitely some wisdom to this, but I think acceptance can be problematic. Believers should enjoy peace no matter our conditions, which is a form of acceptance, but it's a form that has more to do with knowing grace in imperfect situations than with accepting that situations are unchangeable. We're at peace whether the healing succeeds or fails, but that doesn't mean we can't try. Grace, not fatalism, is the key.

I'm often called to try last-minute healings at deathbeds. If I fail, I don't talk about acceptance; instead, I talk about grace—about how God has a solution even for the tragedy of death. If I can't heal the body, God can still heal the soul. If not one manifestation of grace, then the next. The only thing we have to accept is God.

Part of accepting God means accepting my shortcomings. If I'm sharing the gospel with a nonbeliever in my office and the person is unmoved, I don't restrain the person and insist that conversion happen before he or she leaves. Instead, I bless the person as he or she goes and trust God's grace to reach this individual some other way. Conversion always should happen, but I recognize that it doesn't. Similarly, at deathbeds, perhaps healing should happen, but I won't lock the doors and insist I be allowed to minister until the coroner comes. I try hard, and then I walk away in the confidence of grace. That's about the best way I know to describe it.

I remember being called to minister to a very elderly church member with irreparably failing lungs. The doctors told her family that if they took her off the respirator, she would die within a day, but the old girl was tired of the hospital and wanted to go home. I didn't know her family, but they called me to come to the hospital as they took her off the machine. I did my ministry and then, having no immediate evidence of healing, I spoke about heaven and kissed her as I left. As it turned out, she miraculously recovered and lived several more years, which gave her family a wonderful experience of God's power. But I'd like to think her family would have had an experience of God's grace either way.

Getting Started

At my church we have a saying: "We're in it for the stories." It really has two meanings.

First, the wealth of following Jesus is often best expressed by the stories we have to tell. Jesus promised us abundant life, which means we should have a great richness of experience. Accordingly, folks from our church sometimes celebrate simply by gathering to share recent and gripping stories. There's never a shortage, and supernatural experiences usually figure prominently.

Second, we understand that our stories are actually a foundation for practicing our ministries. Our stories of healings help empower our healing ministry because when one person shares a testimony about a healing, the next person will have more faith to try healings. This is growth.

The best way to get started in healing ministry is to jump in, but, as you start, one of your first goals should be to generate a few healing stories. Once you have just a few, you can wield your ministry more prominently because the stories will help you engage people and spread the faith you'll need to go forward.

To start collecting testimonies, I recommend that you start healing ministry in homes or small groups as people learn the basics and get going. Jesus' first healing was in a home with Peter's mother-in-law. When that story got out, crowds immediately came as a result, and they came with some faith and excitement. One small victory empowered expansion.

At some suitable point you'll want to become very public about healing ministry. You'll want your church to be known as the healing church. You'll want a culture of healing in which many pull together in faith, obedience and consecration, and in which many gifts are leveraged—so that many may come and receive.

And when they do come, may it be said of us, as it was of him, that "many followed" and "all were healed."

So Much Loving Me

Several years back I was invited to a week-long Christian gathering in Bangladesh. The plan was for me to do a little sharing and to minister supernaturally to a group of young Bangladeshis who had become interested in Jesus. Some young people from my church traveled with me, and I told them that they would serve as my ministry team. None of them had much experience in supernatural ministry, but they were game to try.

We spent a wonderful week exploring God through Scripture, worship and experience. Bangladesh suffers from some of the world's worst poverty, but its people are strikingly hospitable and affectionate. We made a lot of close friends.

On our last day we ended by praying together for the power of the Lord. Our team began moving among the young Bangladeshis, laying on hands and seeing power flow. A few of the Bangladeshis were filled with the power of the Spirit and began speaking in tongues. A few others were healed of various infirmities. The Spirit fell upon a group of young Bangladeshi women in a profound way, and they all at once began weeping with great passion for their people. It was heavenly.

Out of the corner of my eye I saw a young man collapse to the ground. I knew from a previous interaction that he was a teenager and had just started following the Lord. My friend Will moved to minister to him, so I turned to attend to someone else. A minute later, Will tapped my shoulder and nodded toward the guy on the floor. "Jordan," he said, "what do you think about that?"

Will and his wife had joined our fellowship a year earlier. He was twenty-four and had what you might call a life of hard knocks. He had not been active in church before, but as we studied the Gospel of Mark together, he got a riveting picture of Jesus. He was excited to think that the kingdom could make a difference to people in the here and now, and he had come on the trip in hopes of seeing the sort of things he had read about in Mark's Gospel. Sure enough, what he was seeing at that moment was a full-on demonic manifestation.

The young man he was ministering to was writhing on his back in a sort of semi-conscious state. It looked like all the blood had drained from his face. He grunted some unusual sounds and every once in a while gagged strenuously. It wasn't pretty.

"Yeah, well, that's a demon," I told Will.

He looked at the kid and then back at me, and I could read in his face the collision of several urgent thoughts.

"Will, you know this," I said. "Go cast it out!"

In a moment that I'm pretty sure changed his life forever, Will spun around, strode over to the young man and confidently issued orders: "In the name of Jesus, get out of him! You evil spirit, leave!"

At that the kid began vomiting an immense amount of inexplicably bright yellow fluid. It looked a bit like the antifreeze fluid you put in car radiators. It poured over the concrete floor, and some of the other young Bangladeshis grabbed a few old newspapers and spread them out to sop it up. When the vomiting stopped, the young man became peaceful and opened his eyes. It was over.

Through an interpreter the teen eventually shared a few details. Until becoming a believer, alcohol abuse had dominated his life. When the demon began manifesting, he didn't know what was happening, but when he vomited the strange fluid, he said, it tasted just like the wine he used to drink back in his village. He hadn't had any wine for weeks, but the taste was unmistakable. No one could explain the freakish yellow color of the fluid; nothing yellow had been served recently at the gathering. But, clearly, the kid had been delivered from a demon of alcoholism.

We listened further as the young man's testimony was translated to us in broken English: "I believe in Jesus before, but now I think he is so much loving me." That young fellow is now serving Jesus fulltime as a minister in his country.

Later that afternoon, I chatted with Will about the day.

"So, that's how it happens," he said.

"Well, that's one way."

"It's different from just reading about it," he said, "But it's kind of the same too."

"Yep."

He paused. "Man, I kind of feel like I just want to keep doing this."

"I hear you."

"You know," he said finally, "I just feel like Jesus really loves these people."

"Yeah," I said, "I know."

Will and his wife spent the next three years preparing themselves for international service and then went to work for an aid agency in Bangladesh. Then, through one prophetic dream and an extraordinary series of unlikely events, Will became the coach of the national squash team of Bangladesh. He still lives and serves "in the country Jesus loves."

The Ministry of Deliverance

Of all supernatural ministries, deliverance is probably the most unsettling and provocative. A person can believe in God and still often pass as a balanced person. Someone can even pray for the sick and, as long as he or she doesn't push it too far, be quite welcome in polite company. But once we start trying to cast demons out of people, we've definitely left the standard orbit of respectability.

Demons are even out of fashion among many believers. Churches often preserve a hint of healing ministry in their liturgies, but it's difficult to find any traditional expressions of deliverance ministry. In prayer circles I sometimes find warriors praying against demonic principalities in their city or nation, but it's rare to see them actually driving demons from people. When I speak at Christian conferences in the West, I'll often ask, "Who here thinks there are demons in the world?" and I find almost every believer does, in principle. Then I'll ask, "Who has ever tried to cast a demon out of someone?" and I'll get a few hands at best.

This is pretty interesting, really, because Jesus was probably initially most famous as a deliverance minister. He opened his public ministry by casting a demon out of a synagogue attender, and onlookers exclaimed, "What is this? A new teaching—and with authority! He even gives orders to impure spirits and they obey him!" (Mark 1:27). Jesus then solidified his debut by traveling "throughout Galilee, preaching in their synagogues and driving out demons" (Mark 1:39). Healing ministry came later.

Deliverance was unique to Jesus: the ancient prophets had performed many miracles, but there are zero Old Testament accounts of deliverances. Jesus' "new teaching" was built on the manifest collision of spiritual kingdoms: Satan was getting observably beaten up.

When Jesus sent out his disciples, he "gave them authority over impure spirits. . . . They drove out many demons" (Mark 6:7, 13). There are approximately twenty accounts of deliverances or clusters of deliverances among the Synoptic Gospels, five more in the book of Acts and countless more recorded throughout church history. By all rights, believers should embrace deliverance ministry eagerly.

But while deliverance ministry should be common—indeed, *because* it should be common—I think it's helpful to admit there's a lot we don't know about demons.

Apparently, demons are the part of the ancient angelic race that ruined itself through an unsuccessful rebellion against God (Isaiah 14:12-15; Revelation 12:7-9). God currently allows demons to walk the earth, and God's angels sometimes still fight them (Daniel 10–12), so evidently God has chosen to let their rebellion linger in a way that influences ours. It's clear that demons seek to corrupt us—perhaps because we're made in the image of the God they loathe. Scripture suggests they don't necessarily aim to kill us outright but want to discourage us from trusting God (see Job 1–2).

In contrast, when we humans choose to submit to God, we actually get to apply God's authority over demons: "These signs will accompany those who believe: In my name they will drive out demons" (Mark 16:17). God has complete power over demons, but insofar as the battle against them rages on earth, he lets us enforce his victory.

And that's about all we know.

Deliverance ministry will always seem a little exotic (read "weird") because it's really just our intersection with a battle that extends well beyond us. We fight demons, but we're often ignorant of the backdrop events of the spirit world. There will always be information we don't have, supernatural manifestations that seem bizarre and a keen need to trust the Lord. So, we'd do well to approach deliverance ministry in as humble and uncomplicated a manner as possible.

Accordingly, here's my nutshell description of deliverance basics: Deliverance ministry is warranted when a demon has taken such control over a person that it can maintain a constant grip, actually residing in or on the person. It can be hard to diagnose how demons have gained this influence, but it will somehow involve the sinful surrender of a person's self-control, often due to fear or deception. We usually drive out demons by simply ordering them to go. They obey (grudgingly) if they're convinced that we've developed sufficiently in the Lord's power. A successful deliverance doesn't guarantee the former sufferer will always be secure from demons, but it does provide the person with a renewed ability to make free choices to stay clear of them.

> We usually drive out demons by simply ordering them to go. They obey (grudgingly) if they're convinced that we've developed sufficiently in the Lord's power.

For the rest of this chapter I'll try to lay out the elements of a solid deliverance ministry. I'll start with a point about the nature and personality of demons (since you'll have to interact with them), and I'll talk a bit about how they gain direct control over people. I'll focus on outlining a basic model for the expulsion of a demon from someone, and I'll discuss practical tips for going about the ministry in general: how to decide when to do it, and how to help make sure a person's deliverance is fruitful for the long term.

Creatures, Not Conditions

If we believe in demons at all, then we believe that they're actual beings. It's popular to refer to "demons of the mind" as a way to describe the emotional battles we all fight within ourselves, but when we cast out a demon, we're not fighting an emotional state, a mental illness or even a sinful behavior. We're fighting against an individual spirit-creature with its own personality and attitude. Demons aren't conditions; they're creatures.

That might seem simple enough, but when I train believers in deliverance, they're often eager enough to pray about demons ("O Lord, grant us freedom in our struggle!") or to offer counsel to a demonized person ("Brother, you need to resist in faith"), but they're frequently reluctant to address the demon personally ("Demon, go away, now!"). I guess this isn't terribly surprising because people aren't used to talking to demons. It's awkward. It's freaky. And it can be unpleasant because—surprise!—demons tend to behave badly.

Jesus' deliverance ministry frequently involved disagreeable conversations with evil spirits. The demon in the synagogue shouted, "What do you want with us, Jesus of Nazareth? Have you come to destroy us? I know who you are—the Holy One of God!" It was a combination of taunting and respect. "'Be quiet!' said Jesus sternly. 'Come out of him!'" The spirit wailed loudly in a full-on tantrum as it came out (Mark 1:24-26). That's pretty much the typical pattern: a demon pops up rudely, you tell it to shut up and go away, and the unruly spirit fusses but ultimately leaves.

The most famous Gospel story of deliverance is probably the account of Jesus casting the legion of demons from the suffering man in the region of the Gerasenes (Mark 5:1-20). Hundreds of demons had infested the man and were torturing him endlessly. When Jesus shows up, they protest, "Have you come to punish us before our time?" When Jesus tells them to leave, they don't immediately obey. Instead, they argue and plead that they be allowed to infest a nearby herd of swine. Jesus gives them leave, perhaps to embarrass them, because when the dirty things try to inhabit the pigs, the honest swine drown themselves in the lake instead. Jesus carries the day, but the interaction is enormously messy because the demons are so rancorous and reluctant.

Demons know they must respect God's authority, but they're posturing and petulant. Hollywood sometimes portrays demons as lordly, but in reality demons have the personality and attitude of a spoiled three-year-old child. They pout and fume. They cry, "No fair!" and stamp their feet and throw themselves on the ground. In Bible accounts they often protest, throw fits and obey slowly. Demons might be smarter than the average three-year-old, but a deliverance session isn't a battle of wits; it's a battle of wills. It's less like maneuvering in a courtroom and more like trying to make an elementary-school bully behave. Demons don't resist because they're lordly and intelligent; they resist because they're defiant little creeps.

> A deliverance session isn't a battle of wits; it's a battle of wills.

When I was in graduate school, my wife and I helped plant a church in south Chicago. Gloria, an undergraduate student from a staunchly Buddhist family, started hanging around our fellowship (she had a crush on one of the guys). She was a petite, pretty, very friendly girl who liked to dance at raves. She was drawn to Jesus but couldn't quite accept him as her own. Then one night she ended up at a late-hour worship and prayer gathering, which led to me getting a 3 a.m. phone call from my young friend Pierre.

"Sorry to call so late," he said, "but, um, Satan's speaking to us out of Gloria. Do you think maybe you could come over? Now?"

"Wow. Satan, huh? What exactly is Satan saying?"

"He's saying, 'She's mine! You can't have her!' And it's in this really growly voice. So, yeah, can you come?"

When I first arrived, Gloria seemed fine, so I suggested, "Hey, how about we start by you just declaring that Jesus is your Lord?" She tried, but the demon interjected in a strange voice, "No, she's mine!"

"In the name of Jesus, let her go!" we said. But Gloria just quivered and grimaced.

So, we prayed a bit more and then repeated the command.

"She's mine," the demon protested, but now the voice sounded small and whiny.

"In the name of Jesus, leave right now!" we ordered. Gloria's body jolted, and several of us felt it physically when the demon took off.

Gloria smiled, and the first words out of her mouth were "Jesus is Lord. Jesus is my Lord." And she meant it. She's since become a church planter and a full-time advocate for victims of human trafficking, and is currently attending seminary in New York. (She also married the guy she was crushing on.)

When the group first heard this delicate young woman speaking in a growl, it was shocking. Could it be Satan? But it was just a whiny little demon that hated to see Gloria drawing close to Jesus. When the bothersome spirit fled and stopped interfering, Gloria felt free to move forward with Jesus. The creature was removed, so her condition changed.

Scripture shows that demons can sometimes cause mental or emotional illnesses (the Gerasene demoniac is described as "out of his mind"), as well as physical conditions such as seizures, sensory handicaps, bone deformities and other sicknesses. But it's imperative to understand that while demons might occasionally be involved with psychological or physical pathologies, demons themselves are not pathologies. They're creatures. So, while we might well help sufferers through counseling or clinical therapy, we must also be willing to go directly after the demons if they're there.

How Demons Gain Control of People

Demons are constantly trying to influence us ("the devil prowls around like a roaring lion looking for someone to devour" [1 Peter 5:8]). Our job is to resist. A person will probably need the help of deliverance ministers when a demon has achieved such substantial influence that it can control the person extensively, making resistance extremely difficult. This sort of control involves the demon residing in or on the person, so you can think of it as a sort of infestation, the degree and intensity of which will vary. Indeed, the Greek word that Bible translators often render "possessed" is more literally translated "demonized"—a more flexible term that covers a range of severity. The Gerasene demoniac beat himself, wailed constantly, broke chains with supernatural strength and was "out of his mind." By contrast, the demonized synagogue attender was apparently comfortable and well-behaved until Jesus started ministering. My friend Gloria was strikingly friendly and fun, unaware of her demonic trouble until the voice started speaking through her one night.

But whatever the presentation, it's bad when a demon has such control that it can manipulate a person at will. So, how do demons gain that kind of control over someone?

It's probably worth mentioning that this isn't something Jesus seemed to worry about in the course of exorcisms. When he encountered a demon in someone, he just made it leave; he never bothered to ask how it got there. We don't need to know how a demon took control in order to drive it away. But it's useful to know how demons infest in order to resist them generally, or to help orient a sufferer to deliverance ministry, or to help former sufferers avoid repeat trouble.

Unfortunately, it's hard to say precisely and consistently how demons come to control a human because the avenues and degrees of influence are so varied, and the processes of influence so dynamic. Demons and humans are independent, thinking creatures, so a strategy that demons apply successfully to some individuals under certain conditions might not work with others in different situations. But while we can't deal in formulaic certainties, I can offer some important principles.

To that end, this is the best truism I know: Anything that compromises our capacity for self-control increases demons' capacity to take control. If we can't control ourselves, demons are happy to do it.

....

Anything that compromises our capacity for self-control increases demons' capacity to take control.

....

Demons attack our capacity for self-control by pushing us to sin, and then use the sin to pull our strings until we're so malleable as to be habitable. We don't have to be a particularly great sinner to be demonized; we just have to be accommodating.

When I mention demons and sin, a lot of people think about moral measurement, as if demons are allowed to "claim" people who are judged to be very bad. But the real issue isn't about moral standing; it's about the corruption of our personal control. Demons don't get to infest us because we're bad, per se; they get us because our sin makes it easy for them to control us. Sin itself is a controlling thing, like an addictive drug. It enslaves us piece by piece. When God warns Cain of the dangers of sibling rivalry, he says, "If you do not do what is right, sin is crouching at your door; it desires to have you, but you must rule over it" (Genesis 4:7). In Romans 7:14-20 Paul complains, "I'm . . . a slave to sin. . . . I keep doing the evil I don't want to do! If I do what I don't want to do, it's no longer I who do it, but sin living in me that does it." In Ephesians 4:18, he says that sin "darkened the understanding" of sinners, meaning that sin disables our capacity to tell what's sinful. Sin isn't just a bad choice; it progressively ruins our capacity for choice. Jesus described sinners as being "sick" (Matthew 9:12). Sin weakens us.

Of course, all of us sin, and therefore all lack personal control to some extent, and thus we're all in danger of demonization. But I think things get particularly dangerous when we adjust to our wrongdoing—when, through choice or passivity, we simply allow a certain sin to reign, or we accept it as an inevitability. In doing this we surrender a chunk of control. We might think of "big" sins in this regard, but they're not necessarily the culprits. A man might commit murder and not be demonized through it, while another man who merely frequents pornographic websites might really let the behavior control him to the point of demonization. Again, it's not always about virulence or magnitude; it's about accommodation.

Not all ways of ceding control to sin involve having dark intent. Sometimes we're just beaten down and give in. The Jews of Jesus' day called Satan Beelzebul (Matthew 12:24; Luke 11:15), which means "Lord of the flies." If you've worked a farm, you know that flies swarm to any open wound on the animals. So too demons seek to capitalize on our emotional, mental, spiritual and physical wounds. Injuries can make us particularly susceptible to demons' two biggest weapons of domination: lies and fear.

For example, Paul talks about "deceitful desires"—harmful cravings that seem good to us at the time. Sometimes we embrace them because we choose to lust instead of think (demons and advertising agencies both bank on this). But other times, Jesus says, we're just "lost"—misguided, clueless. Life can knock us around so much that we come to believe deep, disorienting lies about ourselves or God: "You're worthless," "You're hopeless," "God is stingy." If you seek comfort based on your "worthlessness," you'll choose bad comforts. If you don't trust that God is generous, you'll become competitive and greedy.

Demons' two biggest weapons of domination: lies and fear.

Lies do their worst damage when coupled with fear. One of my personal sayings is "Fear is the start of every bad thing." This is because fear kills faith. In faith Peter walked quite well on the waves, until he focused on the storm and became afraid (Matthew 14:30). Faith trusts God in a situation; fear means not trusting him. Where one gains, the other loses. When fear dominates, we chase earthly power, reach for superstitious security, indulge fleshly escapism or just surrender in life. And then we're controllable. So demons whisper to us about fear of rejection, fear of failure, fear of the future—most any fear will do. Jesus, in contrast, commanded us to never worry about anything (Matthew 6:25-34).

In tribal areas of Southeast Asia, where I sometimes minister, many people wear woven bracelets to represent their manacles of bondage to evil spirits. According to legend, tribal ancestors lost their relationship with the Great God, so they voluntarily enslaved themselves to the wicked mountain spirits as a way to keep from being harassed by them. Evil spirits are invited to "own" each newborn, and the children are taught to honor the spirits' power. It's literally a deal with the devil. I think many of us make similar fear-based deals, but with far less awareness. Children are especially vulnerable, not because their sins are great (on the contrary!) but because they lack the awareness to resist sin and dark misunderstandings. Traumatized adults who accept lies out of fear or fatigue can be in the same boat. Others of us just give in to sin, plain and simple, and rationalize it any way we can. However we lose control, the effect is the same.

You might say that our fight against demons is a battle for self-mastery—for the capacity to make free choices based in truth rather than "deceitful desire." It's desperately difficult to live freely—free of fears, lies and sinful trouble—unless you have God's help.

> God doesn't want to control us; he wants to restore our ability to control ourselves.

We're told in Galatians 5 that one of the fruits of the Holy Spirit is self-control. God doesn't want to control us; he wants to restore our ability to control ourselves. To that end, he reveals truth and drives out lies, and his perfect love drives out fear (1 John 4:18). Demons, on the other hand, use lies and fears to tempt us to sin and then control us through it. God strengthens our self-control; demons try to steal it.

How to Do Deliverance Ministry

So, we know that demons are supernatural creatures with the personalities of whiny brats, and they gain control of us through lies, fears and sin. Now, how do we get rid of them?

Technically, deliverance ministry requires three things.

First, we have to *discern the demon's presence.* While we typically know that a sick person is sick, we won't necessarily know that a person is demonized right away because, well, demons are usually invisible and don't always manifest clearly.

Second, we need to *exert authority over the demon* to make it leave. As with all supernatural ministries, the key is having enough power, but with demons it also helps to be stubborn.

Third, we need to discern when the demon has gone.

In terms of actually casting out a demon, that's about all there is to it. So, let's look at those three parts.

How to Tell If It's a Demon

You can discern the presence of a demon in a few different ways: through supernatural revelation, through obvious manifestations or, in a more limited manner, through a person's suspicious behaviors or experiences.

Supernatural revelation can come in two forms: either the Holy Spirit can tell you about the demon, or you can use your own spiritual senses to perceive the demon's presence or activity. Some people can spiritually sense demons the way folks with keen ears can hear extreme frequencies that others miss. This may be what Paul was writing about when he spoke of the gift of "distinguishing between spirits" (1 Corinthians 12:10). We'll talk more about the ministry of supernatural revelation in an upcoming chapter, but it's easy to imagine how useful it can be for perceiving hidden demons that are causing trouble. Sometimes, if we sense a demon and call it out, the demon becomes agitated and manifests in a more obvious way, like a cockroach that scurries noisily when the lights are turned on.

The presence of a demon will be pretty clear to the trained—or even the untrained—eye. If a normally pleasant person interrupts our conversation by suddenly going bug-eyed and shouting "He's mine!" while spit dribbles down his chin, well, that's what we call a sign. Often, agitated demons will manipulate a person's body in strange ways: contortions of face or frame, acts of incredible strength, sudden seizures or inexplicable sensations. These manifestations will be involuntary and can range from outlandishly severe to quite mild. Recently, one of our ministers received a nighttime call from the girlfriend of a man who had started speaking oddly, contorting impossibly and, she reported, levitating off the bed. When our team arrived, the poor man had strained muscles, painfully inflamed joints and impressively swollen extremities. A couple years ago a ministry partner of mine was ministering healing to a ten-year-old village girl with tuberculosis, and a demon manifested so powerfully that it took eight adults to hold her down. After they cast out the demon, the tuberculosis vanished. More mildly, a friend with bronchitis suddenly experienced a numbing coldness and an inexplicable pressure on his back as we tried to heal him. We proceeded to drive away an afflicting spirit and his lungs were immediately healed.

The key to evaluating such overt manifestations is good old common sense. Shouting is not necessarily demonic, but an otherwise normal person who suddenly screams violently whenever you pray for him or her might well be demonized. Seizures are not necessarily demonic, but seizures that only seem to happen during prayer or worship times might well be. You should never jump to conclusions, but neither should you ignore the obvious. In cases in which someone might be manifesting a demon but you're not sure, take the time to pray for revelation and bring your gifts of supernatural discernment to bear. If you're not certain, don't pretend that you are. Seek the Lord for help.

A person's suspicious behaviors or experiences can't confirm the presence of a demon on their own, but they can aid in the discernment process. It's helpful to remember that demons use sins, wounds, lies and fears to gain control over people. So, when I'm ministering to someone who suffers from obvious patterns of sin, striking emotional wounds, profound deceptions or extreme fears, I tune in spiritually.

For instance, people who have embraced drugs or sexual addictions have made themselves particularly vulnerable to demonic control, so, when ministering to them, I keep an eye out for demonic trouble. People who have endured deep emotional traumas, physical abuse or prolonged mental anguish will frequently suffer from consuming fears or compulsive emotional defenses. Since demons often try to capitalize on such things, I stay alert for their presence. People who have been involved in the occult or who have actively worshiped dark religious spirits have effectively invited demons into their lives, so that's a big red flag. Again, none of these behaviors or experiences guarantee demonic involvement, but they warrant sensitivity. Discerning the presence of demons doesn't require paranoia or demon hunting; it just requires awareness.

The best thing you can do to grow in awareness is to develop in God's supernatural power, because the presence of God's power unsettles demons and often provokes them to tip their hand. In Bible accounts, demons often manifested openly just because Jesus showed up. Similarly, in intense worship services, prayer times, healing ministry sessions, moments of prophetic ministry, frontier outreaches or any place where the glory of the Lord is particularly evident, demons are more likely to "out" themselves somehow. So, if you want to grow in discernment experience, it's good to be a powerful believer in the company of powerful believers doing powerful kingdom things.

How to Make Them Leave

Once you've identified a demon, then what? A demon usually won't leave a person just because it's been revealed. Most of the time we have to step up and make them leave. But you can't physically grab a demon and toss it out. Instead, you'll notice that Jesus and his disciples typically ordered them out, meaning that the demons were somehow convinced they had to leave.

What convinces them? Well, since demons have to respect God's authority, they'll obey us when they're convinced we move in God's authority. Fortunately for us it turns out that demons are fairly discerning, meaning that if you flow in a lot of God's supernatural power—if you're a person of extreme obedience, faith and consecration—demons will sense it easily enough.

In the Gospels, demons were able to recognize Jesus' authority from a long way off (Mark 5:6-7), and later it's clear they could recognize the kingdom authority of Christian ministers just by observing them (for instance, during Paul and Silas's visit to Philippi in Acts 16). In Acts 19, when non-Christian priests tried unsuccessfully to cast out a demon by invoking the names of Jesus and Paul, the demon replied, "Jesus I know, and Paul I know about, but who are you?" (v. 15). Demons seem to have a pretty solid idea of who has enough power to order them around, and who doesn't.

So, in theory, if you're a person who has developed in God's supernatural power and authority, you should find it easy to get demons to obey you. But let me mention a couple wrinkles.

First, demons are uncooperative creatures: they know they have to obey, but they will resist petulantly. So, deliverance ministers sometimes have to go through bothersome contests of convincing. Demons tried to argue and negotiate with Jesus on occasion (recall how the legion of demons fussed until Jesus allowed them to flee into the pigs; Mark 5:1-13), so we can certainly expect them to argue, throw tantrums and try to intimidate us. None of these antics necessarily means that we lack the power to drive the demon out; they just mean that the demon is a stubborn little brat. The thing to do is to stick with it.

Usually, deliverance sessions are fairly quick, but I've taken part in some that have lasted many hours. When this happens, I might take breaks for a little worship or prayer (to both refresh me and to intimidate the demon), and then simply repeat my commands with unchanging conviction: "Demon, Jesus is Lord, and it's time for you to go. Now!"

Demons sometimes try to assert rights to their victims by saying things like "He's been given to me!" or "He's just going to keep sinning!" Some ministers play into this nonsense by adopting a legal mindset, believing the victim must methodically renounce sins or "generational curses" (sins of ancestors) or "religious pledges" (involvement with false gods) before demons are obligated to leave—as if a person needs to be legally qualified to receive God's mercy. In Scripture, we never once see Jesus or other ministers ask people to renounce their sins before an exorcism. Indeed, if a demoniac is "out of his mind" or manifesting dramatically, it might be impossible to talk with the person about repentance until after the demon goes!

I remember a ministry gathering near San Francisco at which a lovely, well-spoken young lady approached me for prayer about her nagging depression. When I began praying, she fell backward, screamed and began wildly punching herself in the face—a graphic manifestation of a spirit of shame. In the midst of that violence it would have been ridiculous to try to talk to her about shame or shameful behavior. Instead, we drove the demon out and then ministered to her when things were quiet.

In any case, forgiveness is a ministry of mercy, not a legal transaction. In Mark 2 Jesus tells the paralytic, "Son, your sins are forgiven" before the man says a word. On the cross Jesus says, "Father, forgive them" while they were killing him. And Jesus gives his disciples the ministry of forgiveness: "Whomever you forgive is forgiven indeed" (John 20:23, my translation). God's grace empowers us to forgive people of their sins even before they repent. Demons

would love to convince us that a sufferer hasn't repented well enough
to be freed, but deliverance isn't about the person's legal standing;
it's about whether we've developed enough godly power to chase the
demons away.

That said, I often have sufferers repent of sins or renounce demonic involvements during a deliverance session—not because it's
a legal requirement but because it can increase our supernatural
power for ministry. When a person repents or renounces lies and
fears, it amounts to an act of faith and obedience, and faith and obedience increase the flow of God's supernatural power in us. So, by all
means encourage repentance if you can, because it will only help,
but never let demons pretend they're entitled to stay because
someone hasn't repented well enough. That's just a false excuse.

Twenty years ago, when I knew next to nothing about deliverance, a buddy of mine was struggling with a homosexual sex addiction that had locked him into a promiscuous lifestyle he hated.
He humbly confessed the situation to a few of us and joined a
prayerful sexual recovery group through which he dedicated
himself to purity and accountability. Then, one weekend, while we
were at a Christian conference, he tapped me on the shoulder and
said, "I think God told me you should pray for me about my stuff
right now." We found a space in an adjacent room, and I put a hand
on his shoulder and started praying. He promptly passed out and
twitched on the floor for an hour while I rebuked what I guessed
was a demon. When he woke up, his extreme sexual impulses were
gone. Apparently, part of his trouble had been caused by a controlling spirit. He continued in his recovery group, and today he
and his wife are both powerful recovery ministers. Demons of
sexual addiction are often tough to cast out, but when a person is
as repentant, obedient and faith-filled as my friend, deliverance
gets a lot easier—even for young, clueless ministers.

By contrast, a few years back a friend at another church asked me to pray with him about his insecurity. He was a muscular, stylish fellow who had overcome a childhood handicapped by obesity and social rejection. As I prayed for him, his body shook and he felt sick, and it became clear that his struggle was linked to a demonic presence. Just to make it easier, I invited him to repent of any way he had chosen vanity in his life.

"Do you mean that I have to stop working out?" he asked.

"Well, probably not. But can you just confess that you don't have to be good-looking to be acceptable to God."

To my surprise, he said, "No! I don't want to be ugly."

Ultimately, he actually accepted the demon—which was physically hurting his body at that moment!—rather than accept the idea that he needn't be physically attractive. I had to quit the session until later.

People don't have to repent to be delivered, but it can help the flow of power if they do, and it can sometimes reduce the flow of power if they expressly do not.

> People don't have to repent to be delivered,
> but it can help the flow of power if they do,
> and it can sometimes reduce the flow of
> power if they expressly do not.

Finally, in deliverance, as in all supernatural ministries, techniques can vary, so you shouldn't ever let technical issues complicate your faith. Demons obey you when they encounter godly power in you; how you go about applying that power is secondary.

The most direct way to dismiss a demon is to give a verbal command: "Demon, in the name of Jesus, leave and never return!" This is straightforward and takes absolutely no training, so I like it.

However, anything you do that intimidates the demon will work. Think of an adult with an unruly child. Sometimes the adult gives the kid an order; sometimes the adult will simply look intently at the kid and point to the corner. In Ephesus, demons fled from people who touched cloths that Paul had touched (Acts 19:11-12). Evidently, the scent of Paul's power intimidated them away. In Luke 13 Jesus frees a demonized woman by simply saying, "Woman, you are free of your infirmity" (v. 12). The demon took the hint.

Some believers worry about how to refer to the demons they're addressing. Do you call it a spirit of affliction or a spirit of sickness? Are we casting out a spirit of shame, a spirit of rejection or a spirit of depression? Really, titles just aren't that important. Demons don't listen because you know their names; they listen because you have power. If you want to call one Mr. Ugly, feel free. Jesus often referred to them according to the condition they were linked to. For example, when freeing the deaf and mute boy, Jesus said, "You deaf and mute spirit, come out of him!" The demon got the message. Other times Jesus simply spoke to the "unclean spirit" or "evil spirit" in someone. Only once, when casting the horde of demons from the Gerasene demoniac, did Jesus seek a more precise name. There were so many demons that Jesus effectively asked for a team name for ease of reference. They said, "You may call us legion," and that served well enough (Mark 5:9).

> Demons don't listen because you know their
> names; they listen because you have power.

Remember, don't let technique throw you. If you have a great deal of supernatural power from the Lord, then perhaps just seeing you lay a hand on a person will make a demon flee (the demon knows what's coming). If the Holy Spirit shows himself powerfully in a room, demons will sometimes manifest and let go of people without any intervention (I've seen it often). On the other hand, a demon will sometimes resist even a straightforward verbal command if it doesn't feel compelled by your level of power in Jesus or if it's just being a brat. If that happens, just don't make the mistake of thinking your technique is the problem.

What if you try vigorously to make a demon leave and, at the end of the day, it just won't go? As with unsuccessful attempts at healing ministry, ministers should develop more power and then return to try again. When Jesus' disciples failed to drive the demon from the sick boy, Jesus told them, "This kind [the tough kind] only comes out with prayer and fasting" (Mark 9:29, my translation). In another version, Jesus adds, "It's because you have too little faith!" If Jesus hadn't cast it out, the disciples ideally would have spent some time in consecrated prayer and fasting and then returned to minister to the boy in a situation chosen for its supportive faith environment. That is, they would have worked to increase in power. We should try to build this sort of power awareness and perseverance into both ministers and sufferers. It can be emotionally challenging, but the work of freedom often is.

How to Tell If It's Gone

One expects deliverance sessions to end with a demon leaving, but how can you tell if it does?

Typically you discern a demon's departure in much the same ways you discerned its presence in the first place: through supernatural revelation, obvious manifestations or the victim's experience.

People who have a developed supernatural sensitivity might detect the spirit's departure through a sense of something passing or receding, or by a sudden change in the spiritual environment (a sense that the evil or antagonism ceases).

Other times, physical manifestations of demons' departures will seem pretty clear. In Bible accounts, and in my experience, demons often wail or shriek as they leave people. It typically sounds like screams of frustration or grief, and it's hard to miss. Another manifestation of departure is simply the cessation of manifestations: when a person who is convulsing, grimacing or speaking oddly during deliverance suddenly experiences control and peace, that's a good sign.

Most simply of all, when the demon leaves, the former sufferers almost always know it. They feel a change in their bodies, a sudden clearing in their thoughts and emotions, or a spiritual "lifting." So, if there's uncertainty, ask the person, "What's going on? How do you feel now?" It's a low-tech approach, but very helpful.

In the end, though, the best evidence of deliverance is life change, and common sense is about all one needs to evaluate it. If you cast out a demon of addiction, and the sufferer suddenly finds the capacity to live free of addiction, that's evidence of success. If a person was chronically depressed, but feels more joyful and free following the expulsion of an unclean spirit, that's the right sign. Driving out demons doesn't solve every life challenge, but it should radically improve one's capacity for self-control. A delivered person will still need to make good choices, but should now be able to make them freely.

Practical Ministry Tips

Deliverance is not so much ministry against demons as it is ministry to people in need. Because we're confronting demons, it pays to think like a warrior, but because we're dealing with people in vulnerable situations, it also pays to think like a sensitive shepherd. So, here are a few practical suggestions for finding the best context for doing deliverance and for getting a person through it in a way that leads to lasting life change.

Deliverance is not so much ministry against demons as it is ministry to people in need.

The best times to minister. When should you do deliverance ministry? Maybe you should do it whenever you sense a demon in someone, but if you're one of those people who are extremely sensitive spiritually, you might sense demons almost constantly. I don't have hard data on the distribution of evil spirits, but Jesus and his disciples encountered demons in the streets, in synagogues, on beaches and pretty much everywhere they went. Going after demons can be a little like addressing sins: finding targets can be easy; the real wisdom lies in when and how to deal with them.

Sometimes deliverance needs to be considered in light of larger ministry goals. When Paul and Silas were in Philippi (Acts 16), a slave girl with a fortune-telling demon followed them around shouting, "These men are the servants of the Most High God!" (v. 17). She probably did this to distract and to deceive people into thinking her demon was a righteous herald. Paul and Silas let this continue for days before finally casting out the demon. Why did they wait? Perhaps they realized that just expelling the demon wouldn't fully help the girl or their Philippian outreach. Indeed, the exorcism angered the slave's owners, and the authorities subsequently flogged Paul and Silas and threw them into jail. They escaped miraculously, but they had to leave town without a chance to minister further. So, their patience had bought them a few extra days of evangelism and helped lay the foundations of a church that could help people like the slave girl.

Other times, because deliverance can look and feel dramatic, you might want to adjust your timing to create safety for the sufferer. Public deliverances can be useful evangelistic demonstrations, but, all else equal, we'd like to choose times and places that ensure either privacy or a supportive group environment.

At other times it's wise to wait to do deliverance until you're in a context that will give you the most power. As with healing ministry, an environment of faith is helpful. It's easier to cast demons out in a church than at a drug-flooded concert club. So, if you think you might need a little extra power, there's nothing wrong with being strategic and patient. If a demon pops up during a healing or counseling session, that's typically a fine time to deal with it, and, of course, if God directs me to try deliverance in a given situation, I obey. But, in general, if the situation allows, I'll usher the sufferer to a place or time in which the power of God can flow best.

A general rule: if the power of God is so clear in a situation that it provokes a demon to manifest, then that's probably a good time for ministry because the demon is clearly already intimidated. Again, the more supernatural power you carry, the more often this will happen.

When I was younger, I got to travel on some ministry trips with Steve Nicholson, an experienced power minister and pastor. On one trip we were enjoying a relaxing dinner at the home of our conference hosts. After the meal one of our hosts approached Steve and me and said, "I'm just feeling a bit off. Would you mind praying for me before you leave?" No sooner did we adjourn to the parlor than the fellow started writhing around uncomfortably. Without much ado, Steve followed a prodding from the Lord and said, "Would you like to forgive your father of anything?" The man repented of unforgiveness, and Steve successfully dismissed a tormenting spirit. The whole thing took five minutes, and we seamlessly rejoined the gathering for dessert. It was an odd time to do deliverance, but since the demon was already jittery, the ministry was easy.

Follow through. The whole point of deliverance ministry is to free people to grow with God. So, it's imperative that we help people follow up their deliverance with healthy discipleship.

It's imperative that we help people follow up their deliverance with healthy discipleship.

In Matthew 12 Jesus explains that if a demon leaves a person who does not secure his or her "house," then the demon might return with "seven spirits worse than itself" and infest the person again. Some believers wrongly interpret this teaching as a warning against casting demons out of nonbelievers. Actually, it's a warning against exorcising demons without bothering to tend to the sufferer afterward.

After Mary Magdalene was delivered of seven demons, she became one of Jesus' greatest followers. When Jesus freed the Gerasene demoniac, he instructed the man to tell his story throughout the Gentile Decapolis, making him the very first foreign missionary. Good deliverance ministries will always be marked by their ability to help people follow through with God.

Good follow through is defined by two straightforward questions. First, does the person understand the sins, wounds, lies or fears that got him or her into trouble in the first place? Second, is the person learning how to make godly choices with his or her new freedom?

There are innumerable ways to help a person sort through these issues, but the best general step is the most obvious one: plug the person into a strong community of disciples.

If your church or fellowship is going to be a fruitful discipleship community for those who experience deliverance, you'll have to create an environment in which deliverance has no stigma. If people can't freely share their deliverance testimonies in your community, then it will be hard to help them grow through the experience. And if your community never hears about deliverance experiences, it probably won't ever learn to value them.

The big rule. Invariably, when I teach deliverance seminars, someone will ask, "Don't we need to be careful when we cast out demons so they don't just leave the person and attack us instead?" The question probably comes from watching horror films. The truth is, demons should be afraid of us, not the other way around.

The big rule for fighting demons is this: Never, at any time, in any situation, with anyone, be afraid of a demon. Period.

It would be a great sacrilege to fear demons, because fear is often how demons control us. If you want to protect yourself from demons, be godly, but don't ever let a demon intimidate you, especially not during a deliverance session.

Similarly, we shouldn't fear trying deliverance ministry. There's a possibility we might do it poorly or unsuccessfully, but there's a greater danger in just letting oppressed people go without help. Deliverance ministry will surprise and confuse us from time to time because we're dealing with willful, spiritual creatures. But that just makes it all the more important to wade into the ministry and work things out.

Paul says, "Our struggle is not against flesh and blood, but against the rulers, against the authorities, against the powers of this dark world and against the spiritual forces of evil in the heavenly realms" (Ephesians 6:12). It's a very strange battle, but it's our battle.

Special Delivery

As a kid, I had what I thought of as spiritual radar. For example, I had a keen sense for when someone was lying. Sometimes I dreamed accurately about the future, usually just a few days out, and often about the most random things: I foresaw a certain car break-in, the name of the first single to be released from a future Dolly Parton country music album, and the precise outcome of the legendary 1980 Roberto Duran–Sugar Ray Leonard welterweight championship fight. Weirder still, I occasionally sensed what I feared were evil spirits, sometimes in surprising places. While touring an old California mission when I was eight, I became so anxious about a nasty invisible presence in the sanctuary that I refused to enter. And once in a great while, it seemed to me, God would sort of signal me with bursting thoughts or quick little visions.

Aside from a couple experiences I mentioned to my grandma, I told no one about these things—because even a little kid knows when something sounds crazy.

Then again, I did see my experiences reflected in Scripture. I didn't get a lot of steady "churching" in my early years because my family moved around a lot. (We were hiding from the police, which is a story for another day.) So I mostly explored the Bible on my own, and I noticed that a lot of the coolest Bible stories involved God speaking to someone in dreams, visions or mysterious words. While the churches I encountered all taught those Bible stories, none seemed to expect to experience the things in them. So I stayed mum. I was much older when I finally found a church that worked on hearing the direct, prophetic voice of the Lord.

One summer I went on the first of my many ministry trips with my friend Steve Nicholson, whose church I attended at the time. Steve had been invited to minister supernaturally at a number of churches and conferences in England, and a handful of us traveled with him to assist however we might. Occasionally, during ministry sessions, Steve would ask us if we felt God was saying anything that someone would find useful. I tried volunteering a few things, and Steve made a point to keep asking me for more.

During one gathering of a few hundred folks, Steve paused and asked me to pick the person in the crowd whom I "felt led" to pick, so I asked a woman to stand up.

"Tell her what you see now," he told me.

I eventually said, "Well, ma'am, it's kind of like I see a fruit, a strawberry actually, superimposed over you."

"Describe it," said Steve.

"It's framed in a little circle, as if it were part of a design or maybe a decorative patch."

At this point, the woman closed her eyes and started crying softly.

"Tell her what you think it means," said Steve.

"Well, I think maybe the strawberry represents a promise of fruitfulness for someone in your family," I told her. "I think this promise was there at birth, but the person kind of set it aside. You've been waiting and praying for this person to come back to God. I think

God's saying that now is the time."

Suddenly, a young woman stood up in the back of the auditorium. "I'm her daughter," the young woman said, and she took the scarf off her neck, and pulled back the broad lapel of her jacket. There, underneath the lapel, formerly hidden from view, was a large fabric patch with a bright strawberry on it.

That patch had decorated her favorite overalls when she was a toddler. She'd had a wayward season as a young adult, but during a recent reconciliation visit with her mom, she'd come across the tiny, old pair of overalls while rummaging through the attic. She'd cut off the patch and sewed it on her jacket in remembrance of happier times. Encouraged by that visit with her mom, the daughter had returned to church for the first time that weekend.

"I think that strawberry is a sign that you should be back with the family of God," I said. The young woman nodded vigorously and eventually came forward to receive the help of the Lord. The mom cried, and a few hundred people looked at me as if I knew what I was doing.

Later I told Steve, "That vision worked out well, but even if I 'see' stuff, I'm half-guessing about what it means."

"Well," Steve said, "you might be receiving prophetic information all the time, but not notice it or know how to understand it. How are you going to get better at it if you don't practice?"

The very next day we were whisked to a conference for five hundred Anglican leaders from all over Britain. Five minutes before the start, Steve sidled up to me and said, "So, this conference is about how to develop prophetic ministry in churches!"

Most Anglicans don't have much experience with supernatural ministry, and Steve's job was to convince them to try it.

"I'm going to the podium to talk for about ten minutes," he said, "and then I'm going to call you up, and you're going to prophesy over them for the rest of the hour." Then he giggled wickedly and walked away.

Steve introduced me as one of his "most trusted prophetic advisers," "a young prophet with a long, proven track record," "a seasoned prophetic voice." In other words, he lied. But I stepped up and did my best. A young man had led some songs that afternoon, and I prophesied that his music would become known around the world. It turned out he was already well-known in his region, and in fact he did become an internationally famous worship leader within a few years. I also called out any number of Anglican priests and told them what I sensed were their spiritual gifts, and my words seemed generally accurate and encouraging. But I had one word in particular that I thought would be totally impressive and convincing.

The Lord had given me a strong, definite vision of an elderly woman in white adorned with what looked like a wedding bouquet on her head. I saw her face in detail, and in my mind I clearly heard a voice say, "Her name is Alice. She is not in this room."

I figured that the bouquet represented her marriage-like devotion to the Lord, and I sensed she had never married otherwise. I felt the Lord wanted me to honor her sacrifice of celibacy, which I thought was awesome. The auditorium was jammed with people, so when I heard she wasn't in the room, I reasoned it meant that she was in the overflow room watching the video feed. I would call out her name and her description even before seeing her, and then speak out details about her life after she walked in. The Anglicans would be blown away. I had this one nailed.

"I have a word for someone named Alice, dressed in white," I said into the microphone. "I think you're perhaps in the outer room. Would you come in, please?"

Nothing.

"A word for Alice," I said. "Please come on in, Alice."

Still nothing.

Finally, an elderly man in the front row stood and said, "That's me!"

"Um . . . you don't look like an Alice," I said. "I mean, you know, you're a guy."

"Yes, quite," he said.

I felt the burden of a thousand Anglican eyes watching me botch a prophecy and embarrass a perfectly nice old man. It turned out he was hard of hearing and misheard the name I had called out. I eventually exited the stage ingloriously, without finding Alice, surely having wounded the cause of prophecy in Britain.

That night I went with Steve and a few others to minister at a very old church in London. We got there early, and as I watched the church leaders trickle in, an elderly woman arrived. I recognized her immediately. She walked over and said, "Hello, my name is Alice."

We sat together and chatted before the meeting started. I didn't tell her about my earlier experience, but just listened to her talk about her life. She had served in international missions and had never married. "I didn't get a wedding," she said, "but I got Jesus!" Every detail panned out: her face, her name, her dress, her marital devotion to the Lord. And, precisely as the Lord had told me, she hadn't been there in the room earlier that day.

"I heard your team was ministering in prophecy at Chorleywood, but I wasn't able to get there for the session," she said.

"Yes, ma'am, I know," I admitted sourly. "But I think maybe the Lord has arranged for you to receive a prophecy through special delivery."

"Oh, I love to see young people listening to the Lord!" she said.

"Well, apparently, I have a lot to learn about how that works," I complained.

"Then the Lord will teach you!"

The Ministry of Prophecy

If you're relating to a supernatural being, then you should probably expect to have supernatural conversations with him. The Bible makes this pretty clear. Noah, Abraham, Moses, Joshua, Samson, Deborah, Gideon, Samuel, David, Elijah, Elisha, many of the kings, all the recorded prophets of the exile era, Mary and Joseph, Jesus, the Twelve, the woman at the well, Paul, Barnabas, Cornelius, Timothy and oh-so-many others were directed by personal, supernatural revelations. And the New Testament's histories and pastoral writings assure us that God is speaking today just as he always has.

But really, that's not the point. The practical point of prophetic ministry is less about God speaking and more about the development of our listening.

> Prophetic ministry is less about God speaking and more about the development of our listening.

God tends to make himself accessible but not obvious. So, though God speaks, you might not catch it, and if you do catch it, you might not understand it fully. For most of us the process of listening usually happens somewhere amid the pressures of life, so it takes focus. You might associate prophetic revelation with contemplative monks sitting on mountaintops, but for ministry-minded kingdom believers, it's often more like military communications during a battle.

But if prophecy isn't obvious, how can you tell when God's speaking to you? How can you be sure you're not making it up? If prophecies involve symbols and signs, how do you go about understanding them? If life is noisy and prophecy is subtle, what can you do to hear God better?

I'll try to get to it all in steps. For orientation, we'll first talk about the place and nature of revelation in our day. Next, we'll look at how one actually goes about perceiving supernatural revelations, and then we'll talk about how to understand them. Finally, we'll discuss how to use prophecy well—how to apply it sensitively for encouraging people and gathering seekers. I'll close with a few tips on how to get started and grow in prophetic ministry in your church or fellowship.

Revelation Today

The Bible is packed with stories about prophetic ministry, but, as skeptics sometimes argue, spiritual conditions were different back then, and we should expect things to work differently now. And indeed, I think prophetic ministry is different now: it's more plentiful and easier to do safely and well.

In ancient times the Holy Spirit made only cameo appearances. He "hovered over the waters" in the beginning, and was surely active behind the scenes. But with respect to all the indwelling and empowering stuff he does, the Holy Spirit "came upon" only a handful of individuals each generation.

These individuals became known for their special supernatural abilities. They were called prophets, seers or sometimes just "the man of God." Sometimes ancient Scriptures speak of small bands of prophets working together (for example, Elijah and Elisha's "company of prophets" [2 Kings 2:3-7]), but such groups were small and exclusive.

Then, around six hundred years before Christ, the prophet Joel foresaw a day when all people could have access to the supernatural empowerment of the Holy Spirit:

> And afterward,
>   I will pour out my Spirit on all people. . . .
>   [Y]our old men will dream dreams,
>   your young men will see visions.
> Even on my servants, both men and women,
>   I will pour out my Spirit. (Joel 2:28-29)

According to Joel, the immediate hallmark of this outpouring is that everyone—old and young, men and women—would be able to receive direct revelations. When this outpouring of the Holy Spirit finally came to the disciples after Jesus ascended (Acts 2:1-4), a new era began, and according to Scripture we should now expect, among other things, a great multiplication of revelation among the people. Everybody can now be "online."

This not only has huge implications for how each individual walks with the Lord, it also makes prophetic ministry a lot easier to learn and manage.

Since whole groups can now hear from the Lord together, one person's revelation can now be confirmed (or questioned) by other sensitive people around them. We prophesy together, discern together and learn together. As Paul told the Corinthians, "Two or three prophets should speak, and the others should weigh carefully what is said" (1 Corinthians 14:29). It's the rule of confirmation.

The rule of confirmation takes some of the pressure out of the revelation business. In the old days, claims of prophetic revelation were extraordinarily serious business: if a supposed prophet was found to be inaccurate in his declarations or predictions, the people had orders to put him to death (Deuteronomy 18:20). This rather tight editorial control was necessary because the people had no accessible way to check a prophet's authenticity. There were few established Scriptures to check prophetic words against, and there were few other prophets to confer with. But these days anything a believer prophesies can be checked generally against scriptural wisdom and then perhaps specifically by other prophetic believers. We should encourage prophetic ministry in all quarters because it's now possible to have it in all quarters, and because we want lots of good prophetic ministers ready to help one another discern and learn. Today, instead of one small company of prophets, we can have countless communities in which prophetic ministry develops. We can develop individuals who are particularly gifted in prophecy, but also, as Paul suggests, we want to encourage whole churches to be fluent in the ways of prophecy (1 Corinthians 14:1-5). It all makes for uniquely empowered faith fellowships.

A bit before we started the young church I lead, the Lord began speaking to me, out of the blue, about ministry to victims of the sex slave trade. I started researching the vicious business. Then, several other people in our fellowship independently had dreams and visions about rescuing human trafficking victims. With this confirmation we felt compelled to work together. So we hit the streets to pray and make connections in the brothel areas of our city, and we started a safe house. In our first two and a half years as a church, our team helped over forty women and underage girls to get out of the sex industry in our city, and we helped rescue and repatriate victims of international trafficking. Our members also played crucial roles in passing our state's first ever anti-human-trafficking law. We've baptized a number of former victims who have blessed us profoundly. Seeing all this gives us a sense of gratitude, but witnessing all this because we heard the Lord together gives us a sense that God himself is leading our church. That makes us feel ready for anything.

The Practice of Prophetic Ministry

Of course, for individuals or groups to develop well in prophetic ministry, they'll probably have to work at it a bit—and not just at perceiving supernatural information but also at understanding it and applying it to life. We want our revelations to actually produce fruitfulness. To that end, here's a bit of guidance I've found to be helpful: It's relatively easy to perceive a prophecy, harder to understand it accurately and harder still to use it well. We'll want to develop in all three areas.

Step 1: Perceiving a prophecy. Scripture suggests that supernatural revelation can happen in a ton of different ways, and God even seems to like being creative (I mean, a burning bush?). The Lord might speak to you in an audible voice as he spoke to Moses on Sinai (Exodus 33), or you might have an experience in which your spirit seems transported to a different place (Ezekiel 40; Revelation 1), or you could receive a prophetic message from an angel (Daniel 10:4-14; Luke 2:8-10). Judging from Scripture and experience, you'll more commonly perceive revelation through visions or impressions in your mind, or through prophetic dreams during sleep (Jeremiah 1:11-16; Luke 4:1; Daniel 2).

The Bible uses a rich variety of language to describe the experience of revelation: "The word of the Lord came to me." "The hand of the Lord was upon me." "I beheld a vision." "I was in the Spirit." "I saw." "I heard." "I perceived." The point, I think, is to be open. And when I say "open," I also mean "sensitive," because one of the surprises about prophecy is that it is often subtle and puzzling.

If God speaks to you in an audible voice, that would be hard to miss, right? Well, maybe not. When the young Samuel heard God speak audibly to him in the night, he mistook the voice for that of his guardian, Eli the priest (Samuel 3). When the Lord spoke audibly from heaven to affirm Jesus' prayer in John 12:28-29, some mistook the voice for thunder, and others thought it was an angel. We might think a manifest visitation would be easy to identify, but when Joshua encountered "the captain of the Lord's hosts" on the plains of Jericho, he mistook him for a Canaanite soldier (Joshua 5:13-14). And when Jeremiah started having visions as a young man, the Lord initially had to prompt him: "Jeremiah, what do you see?" (Jeremiah 1:11). Often, the trick isn't in perceiving a revelation, but in realizing you've perceived a revelation.

Noticing. I was taught this saying, "Eighty percent of prophecy is just noticing." Sure, if God speaks to you audibly or sends the angel Gabriel to deliver a message, there's reason to think you'll notice something right away. But the more typical sort of visions, dreams and impressions tend to be gentle.

When people ask me what it's like to get a vision, I tell them to try to remember the face of a childhood playmate. Most of my visions are like that—like having an image in my mind of something I used to see. The image may not be crisp, but I know what it is, and there's often an emotional or narrative sense about it—as if it has a tiny bit of story attached to it. So, it's both subtle and rich. I could easily overlook it, but having noticed it, I realize there's quite a bit to it. That's the best way I can describe it.

A prophecy doesn't have to be a visual image, of course. It can be a word or phrase that emerges in your mind, or just some sudden knowledge or conviction that comes from nowhere but seems alive—as if you'd arrived at a conclusion but can't trace how. That is, a prophecy can seem an awful lot like what you might call a special thought. It has some heft, but it's in no way overwhelming. And the trick will be to notice it and identify its purpose.

The same idea about noticing applies to dreams, which we all have every night but tend to dismiss. When I was in grad school, my wife, Sonya, dreamed that we had moved into a large loft apartment with an enormous closet full of vintage costumes. Some days later, while touring her boss's urban mansion, she was shown an upstairs ballroom with a storage room of old costumes. It turned out her boss was thinking of renting the space as a loft apartment, so we moved in. Then, Sonya had a dream about a tree growing from the ballroom floor and sending shoots around our south Chicago neighborhood. We interpreted this to mean that the Lord planned for a ministry to grow from our apartment. We were overbusy and I was fighting a painful health issue, but we started a Bible study for young people, and it soon grew to fill the loft. Then I dreamed that I was driving a maroon-colored convertible packed with our young people up a long hill, and at the top I got out and handed the keys to someone else. Since maroon was the school color at the University of Chicago ("Go Maroons!"), I figured the dream meant that my job was to "drive" this ministry during my grad school years, but then to hand the keys of leadership to someone else. So we led the group until I was almost finished with my degree; then we invited a young pastor to lead it as it opened its doors as a new church (in a neighborhood that really needed one). Over a decade later the church is going strong, and the members of the original Bible study have gone on to plant at least four churches in different places. But here's the thing: it all happened only because Sonya and I bothered to pay attention to our dreams. In any instance we could have just rolled over and gone back to sleep, forgetting the dream.

Familiarity. If most prophecies are this subtle, the million-dollar question is, How can you know for sure that it's God speaking to you? How do you tell a special thought from a random thought? How can you tell a prophetic dream from one caused by the spicy pizza you ate before bed?

Well, there are broad answers that apply. For instance, if a prophecy seems to contradict basic scriptural truths, you can throw it out. Or if you have a predictive revelation or dream that proves factually inaccurate, then you know it wasn't from God and you should discount any other information that went along with it. But these basic guidelines still leave a lot of space for wondering.

So, here's the real key: You discern the voice of the Lord by getting used to the voice of the Lord. That's it.

When I teach about prophecy to live audiences, I always pause and have them close their eyes. Then I ask, "OK, whose voice do you hear speaking at this very moment?"

> You discern the voice of the Lord by getting used to the voice of the Lord.

"Well, yours," they say.

"And how do you know it's my voice?" I ask.

"Because we've been sitting here listening to you," they answer.

"You've listened to me for less than an hour and you can pick out my voice with your eyes closed. Well, many of you have known God for years, so you ought to be able to pick out his voice by now."

Jesus said that the sheep follow the shepherd "because they know his voice" (John 10:4). I could talk to you all day about what it's like to discern a revelation, but when it comes right down to it, it's a matter of experience. Like a mother who can pick the faint cry of her child out of the noise of a crowded playground, I can sift godly impressions out of the noise in my head because I've been focusing on his voice for years. It isn't a formula; it's familiarity. Our God is so relational that it doesn't surprise me that it works this way.

All this makes practice extremely important. At first, when you notice a subtle vision or impression, you'll say, *I wonder if this is prophetic?* or *Could this be from God?* So you'll test it out: you'll seek confirmation from another believer, or you'll actually go pray for the sick woman you've seen in your vision. If what you think you perceived turns out to be accurate and helpful, then bingo, you've just had an experience with the voice of the Lord, and you can register the feel of it.

Telephone versus television. As you practice noticing and discerning revelation, you'll want to bear in mind that not all revelation comes from God speaking to you. Sometimes, you'll know a thing prophetically not because God tells it to you, but because you simply perceive the thing directly with your own spiritual senses. For example, if we're together, God might tell me that you're called to ministry in Calcutta, or I might simply sense a passion in your heart for missions in India. In the former, the Lord gives me a message; in the latter, I just supernaturally observe what's in your spirit.

To illustrate this difference, I like to talk about what I call telephone prophecy and television prophecy. In telephone prophecy the Lord "dials your number" and speaks a message to you. It might come to you as a word, a vision or an impression, but God has sent it specifically to you. It's a personal line. In television prophecy the prophetically sensitive person just picks up spiritual information that's in the air, kind of like how old TV sets picked up the television waves around us, or how radio-telescopes pick up energy waves emanating from cosmic objects. Such waves are always around us, but only certain sensors register them. Similarly, prophetically gifted people—people with exceptional spiritual sensors—can perceive normally invisible information emanating from people and places. The information is always around us, but only some perceive it. Such individuals often seem able to "read" people—to look at them and know things about them: their spiritual state, their spiritual gifts, their degree of truthfulness, the passions of their heart. God doesn't tell them these things; they just sense them.

Paul was probably talking about this sort of supernatural observation when he said that a stranger walking into a group of prophets would have "the secrets of his heart laid bare" (1 Corinthians 14:24-25). It's the sort of thing made clear in 2 Kings 5:26 when Elisha busts Gehazi for lying about taking inappropriate gifts from Naaman: "Was not my spirit with you when the man got down from his chariot to meet you?" says Elisha. God didn't tattle on Gehazi; Elisha simply saw it on his own.

This distinction in perception can be important when you're thinking about what to do with the information you've perceived. Just because I happen to sense that a man on the street has a hidden drug problem doesn't necessarily mean that I should intervene in his life at that moment. However, if God tells me about an individual's drug addiction, then I might infer that he wants me to try to do something about it. When I dreamed the outcome of future boxing matches as a kid, it didn't mean that God was telling me to find a bookie and place a bet; I was probably just picking up bits of the future on my "television set."

Of course, whether I have a personal message from God or merely a supernatural observation, I can follow it up by asking the Lord for advice on how to proceed. In just this way some of my passing television-style observations have helped me intervene against suicides and avoid liars' schemes. However, a very sensitive person—someone with a strong prophetic gift—might get to a point where he or she senses hidden things about almost everyone encountered (which can be emotionally overwhelming), and it will be impossible to follow up on or even to focus on them all. So, part of effective prophetic ministry will be to notice where God directs your attention.

> Part of effective prophetic ministry will be to notice where God directs your attention.

The telephone-television distinction is also helpful when it comes to choosing how to deliver prophecies to people (which we'll discuss shortly). If I share a television observation with someone, it's neither accurate nor helpful for me to preface it by saying, "God says . . ." There's a big difference between saying, "I think God wants me to tell you to move to Calcutta," and saying, "I sense that you have a passion for India. Have you considered ministering there?"

Practiced awareness. In sum, if you want to grow in prophetic perception, you'll want to learn to notice when it's happening. Part of noticing is familiarizing yourself with the feel of the Lord's voice and touch. Another part is staying sensitive to the spiritual information your supernatural senses might pick up around you. Both require practiced awareness. Indeed, more than any other supernatural ministry, I think the ministry of prophecy cultivates in us a constant awareness of the spiritual realm. It encourages us to always be mindful of spiritual things, which makes it a uniquely potent component of the supernatural life.

Step 2: Understanding a prophecy. Alas, perceiving a prophecy doesn't necessarily mean that you'll understand what you've perceived. Prophetic revelation often comes in the form of symbols, signs or riddles that require interpretation—as in "some assembly required." Accurate interpretation is at least as important as sensitive perception.

You'll notice the prevalence of symbols and metaphors in scriptural prophecies. In Isaiah, Jesus is predicted in the form of a dawning light, and the purposes of God are represented by a mighty mountain. In Zechariah, Jesus is represented by a branch, and the sin of the people by dirty garments. God actually ordered Hosea to marry an unrepentant prostitute so that her marital unfaithfulness could serve as a metaphor of Israel's unfaithfulness to God. The book of Ezekiel is so mysteriously symbolic that ancient Israelites were customarily forbidden to read it until they were of mature age. The book of Revelation is so densely symbolic that dedicated people are still arguing today about what it all might mean. On the occasions when the Lord spoke prophetically without a lot of symbolism and mystery, it was considered exceptional: God said of Moses,

> When a prophet is among you,
>   I, the LORD, reveal myself through visions
>   and I speak to him in dreams. . . .
> With [Moses] I speak face to face,
>   clearly and not in riddles. (Numbers 12:6-8)

Happily for us, Scripture also often shows how the old prophets stepped through the process of interpretation. For instance, after God reveals Nebuchadnezzar's dream to Daniel, we get to see Daniel decipher every visual symbol in it (Daniel 2). When Nebuchadnezzar shares his second dream with Daniel, "Daniel . . . was greatly perplexed for a time" (Daniel 4:19) but eventually hammers out the interpretation with the Lord. In the next chapter Daniel methodically interprets the riddle of the writing on the wall for King Belshazzar. In the latter parts of the book, we see angels helping Daniel interpret some of his visions (Daniel 12).

In the early part of the book of Jeremiah we actually get to see God training his prophet in the ways of interpretation. The book opens with the novice Jeremiah claiming to be too young and unsophisticated to be much of a prophet. God responds by taking Jeremiah through a couple of symbolic visions.

"What do you see, Jeremiah?" the Lord asks.

"I see the branch of an almond tree," says Jeremiah.

"You have seen correctly," says the Lord, "for I am watching to see that my word is fulfilled" (Jeremiah 1:11-12).

It turns out that the Hebrew word for "almond tree" sounds like the Hebrew word for "watching." Jeremiah's vision of an almond tree was a visual pun. God was teaching Jeremiah to "get it."

Jeremiah next has a vision of a "boiling pot tilted from the north," which the Lord explains is a symbol for an angry invasion from northern armies. The pot would become a recurring metaphor in Jeremiah's visions (see Jeremiah 18; 19; 22), and thus Jeremiah began to learn his stock symbols.

Most of Jeremiah's subsequent prophecies are recorded as if they came to him as straightforward content, but we do occasionally get to see him work with God on interpretations of symbols such the linen belt (chap. 13), the potter's wheel (chap. 18) and baskets of figs (chap. 24).

Why symbols? If you're like me, you're going to ask why. Why does the Lord so often speak in symbols and riddles? Why not just speak plainly?

Well, there may be several reasons. First and perhaps foremost, symbols and riddles often force a puzzled person to seek God further for help in understanding, which deepens conversation with God, which breeds familiarity with God, which God likes very much. The challenge of interpretation forces us to press into him.

Second, just as a picture is worth a thousand words, symbols are a very efficient way for God to download a lot of rich information. If God spoke prosaically, we'd forget most of what he said, but by speaking in pictures, signs or brief riddles, he helps us remember and consider. For example, in Revelation 5, John describes a vision of a "Lamb, looking as if it had been slain" standing on heaven's throne. The lamb has "seven horns and seven eyes" (v. 6). Well, *thrones* means exalted status. The number seven always represents completion in the Bible, and horns represent governmental authority, so the seven horns speak of total authority. Similarly, the seven eyes speak of an all-seeing quality. So, we're dealing with a superior, all-powerful, all-knowing being. But this figure is also depicted as a puny sacrificial lamb! We're thus provoked to meditate on the matchless humility of the Christ King. John's symbolic snapshot communicates a ton of foundational theology in far less time than it's taken me to write this paragraph.

Third, because we're not used to perceiving stuff in the spiritual realm, I think symbols and signs are often the only way for us to grasp the spiritual information we receive. God's nature is so different from ours that it's probably no wonder the Holy Spirit should appear in the likeness of a dove, that his power should look like tongues of fire, or that a revelation of heaven should be full of symbolic creatures representing unearthly qualities.

Of course, not every prophetic revelation comes as a symbol or metaphor. Sometimes a prophetic direction is very plain: The Lord told Ananias, "Go to the house of Judas on Straight Street and ask for man from Tarsus named Saul, for he is praying" (Acts 9:11). And sometimes prophecies are literally predictive. For example, I dreamed the outcome of the Chicago Cubs' 1996 baseball season right down to the slightly new design of their uniforms. Ironically enough, it's sometimes the literal revelations that are the most confusing because we wonder if they're symbolic: "Am I dreaming about the actual Chicago Cubs, or is the team a symbol for the city of Chicago?" So, alas, even literal prophecies often end up being a matter of interpretation, and we've got to work to get the feel of it.

So, how does one learn to interpret well?

Breaking the code. There are reasons God wants us to work for interpretations, but he certainly doesn't want to confuse us endlessly, so prophetic symbols are not without logic and consistency. They all make some intuitive sense (a vision of deadly tornadoes and flooding will probably not be a symbol for peaceful times), and they tend to hold their general meaning from prophecy to prophecy (the rainbow was a sign of God's promise to Noah, so it will tend to be a sign of promise whenever you see it in a vision or dream). Interpretation is not an exact science, because it involves a very creative God, but learning to interpret is a little bit like learning to read a code, and I can at least offer a few tips in terms of general approach.

> Prophetic symbols are not
> without logic and consistency.

Learning the alphabet. When God called Jeremiah as a prophet, he first introduced Jeremiah to some symbols and how they work. It was like an elementary alphabet lesson. To be a fluent reader of prophecies, you'll want to learn your alphabet of symbols and types of symbols.

You'll probably find that revelations use two kinds of alphabets: one biblical and one personal.

The biblical alphabet is simply the storehouse of symbols drawn from biblical prophecies and stories. The Bible is the world's richest mine of symbols, and Bible familiarity is vitally important to good interpreters. Most believers already know a bit of the biblical alphabet—if we see an idyllic garden, an ark, a sea parting, a giant, the number seven, a cross or a lamb, we'll probably have some idea how to interpret it, so it makes sense for God to use Bible symbols. If I'm puzzled by a symbol in a dream or vision, I'll ask myself if it reminds me of anything in the Bible. Even if my symbol isn't an exact match for a biblical one, I often get interpretive insight: a skyscraper is not exactly like the Tower of Babel, but they're similar enough that I might suspect the modern tower represents human pride in much the same way that the ancient one did.

Your personal alphabet includes symbols or signs that may be unique to you. For instance, I often have dreams that take place in my dad's backyard workshop. Invariably in these dreams there will be an array of symbolic objects laid out on the workbench, and sometimes an angelic figure will explain their meanings or ask me questions about them. In other words, my dad's workshop is a symbolic setting that tells me that God wants me to work on understanding certain lessons or situations in my life.

Over time, I've learned many dozens of personal symbols that God uses to speak to me, though sometimes it's been an awkward process. Beginning in my twenties, I would often see visions of a tin can when I prayed over people. Often the can would have something inside it, but I just couldn't figure out what the can meant. Was God saying that the person needed to be filled like a container, or that the person was in danger of getting rusty? Finally, while praying for a person one day, I had a vision of the tin can and ignored it in frustration. Then I found myself praying, "Lord, please show Eric what he can do to minister well in his situation." Then it came to me. The tin can is a pun/symbol that represents what a person *can* do—the stuff that God specifically empowers. If I see a can with a paintbrush in it, it means you can do art especially well. If the can is filled with money, then you can count on the Lord providing the resources you need for whatever you're considering. It took me three years to figure out that symbol! (Did I mention I have a Ph.D.?)

In shorter order, I learned that feathers are my symbol for prophecy or prophetic gifting, that eyeglasses or contact lenses represent a change in life vision, and that doorways often symbolize choices. I've learned countless other symbols in the course of a years-long conversation with God, and now they're unmistakable to me, even if they stumped me for a while. As you develop your conversation with God, you'll probably get some personal symbols of your own. My friend Jen often dreams about food, and she's learned that the different ingredients in her dream dishes each have unique meanings. My friends in the villages of Bangladesh have rich alphabets based on the elements and implements of river fishing, presumably because that's the context of the daily lives.

Symbolic alphabets can contain more than just visuals or words. Physical sensations are a good example. Sometimes at church one of our ministers will experience sympathetic pain—an acute bodily sensation which reveals that someone present has a problem in that specific body area. We'll interpret the sensation and call it out—"Is there someone here with sharp pain in the left hip?"—and usually someone responds and gets healed. At other times, prophetically sensitive ministers might discern the presence of an evil spirit by way of a physical discomfort, or they might sense someone's inner emotional state by way of sudden, sympathetic emotional surges of their own. These sorts of sensations are simply signs—things you'll notice and learn to decipher through repetition and familiarity.

Symbols in context. Sometimes revelation will come in the form of a single symbol that conveys what you need to know: Jeremiah saw an almond branch and came to understand that the Lord was watching Israel. Other times, revelation comes as a flow of symbols or as layers of metaphors: King Nebuchadnezzar dreamed of a heavenly messenger cutting down a spreading tree, binding its stump in iron, giving it "the mind of an animal" and leaving it exposed to the weather for "seven times" (Daniel 4). Daniel interpreted the tree to be Nebuchadnezzar himself, the "seven times" of exposure and beastliness as a curse of seven coming years of severe mental illness, and the iron-clad stump as a sign the Lord would secure Nebuchadnezzar's throne until he could reclaim it after his years of travail. Daniel had to string the symbols together to get the full narrative sense of the prophecy.

When symbols flow together, it's important to consider them together. Context matters. Rain will symbolize one thing when it's falling gently on the prairie, but quite another if it's soaking someone in a cold nightscape. Since Eden, snakes have symbolized deception, but in Numbers 21, during a plague of snakebites, God told Moses to raise a bronze snake on a pole in order that all who saw it would be healed. So, snakes might represent a deceptive attack, or in a different context they could be about the healing that comes from exposing deceptions.

Usually, when symbols flow together, they simply modify or add to one another. A car might symbolize your life direction. If your dad is driving your car, it might speak of the direction he provides to you. If the car is white, it might speak of God's true direction for you; if it's black, it might speak of a deceptive or hidden direction you should be mindful of. If the car drives into a parking lot, it might speak of you finding a place in a community or organization.

The general rule is to find the story that the symbols tell when taken together. I find it helpful to consider the overall theme of a vision or dream before I focus on any one symbol within it. If I can get a sense for the theme, then the individual symbols become easier to crack.

Workshopping. Since all Christians draw from the same Bible, and since we tend to share general life circumstances with those around us, it's likely that any selected group of people will share many symbols or types of symbols in common. For instance, vehicles almost universally represent life direction in some way: a ship on the ocean might represent direction through uncertainty (because oceans lack fixed points of reference), an airplane might speak of spiritual direction (because it travels through the heavens), a bicycle might symbolize a direction for which you're required to exert yourself. Places of residence or business typically represent the state of our lives: an airport might speak of spiritual transition; a hotel might speak of a temporary condition. And so forth.

Since our prophetic alphabet won't be entirely foreign to others, it means that we can help each other with puzzling interpretations. At my church we call this workshopping. If one of us is stuck on an interpretation, he or she describes the prophecy to the group and we try to work it out together with the Lord. Among other advantages, it's a great way for the more mature prophetic ministers to help the younger ones.

Keeping God in the process. You can find prepared encyclopedias of symbols and their supposed meanings (such books date back at least to the ancient Babylonians), but I typically don't recommend them—partly because symbols and signs can be very personal and are conditioned so heavily by context, but also because interpretation is part of a dynamic conversation with the living God, and thus is best developed through direct interaction with him. When deciphering dreams, Joseph the patriarch said, "Do not interpretations belong to God?" (Genesis 40:8). Part of the process of interpretation, and a big part of its blessing, is the back-and-forth you'll have with the Lord about it. Through that process, you'll find yourself developing a greater working intimacy with God.

Step 3: Using prophecies well. Even if you figure out what a given prophecy means, you'll still have to figure out how to apply it to life or ministry, and this is often the trickiest part. Sometimes it's tricky because the prophecy is symbolic, and symbols just don't lend themselves to precise direction. Other times, though prophecies provide us with enough information to act, they don't provide us with all the information we'd like to have, or will ultimately need down the line. Individual prophecies are usually guideposts, not comprehensive roadmaps. Like much of what God does, revelations typically give us enough to step out in trust, but not enough to be certain. They increase faith; they don't excuse us from exercising it.

To use prophecies well, we'll need humble faithfulness—the ability to act on what we understand without having to pretend we understand more than we do.

Just as you might consult with God while interpreting a prophecy, you'll want to continue to consult with him as you apply it and see things unfold. Humble prophets are open to additional clarification along the way. Prideful prophets think they understand everything, so they miss clarifications as they go and end up confused and angry.

No event in Scripture benefited from more prophetic prediction than the coming of the Messiah, but when Jesus showed up and perfectly fulfilled hundreds of scriptural prophecies, virtually everyone missed it, and most rejected him because they wouldn't give up their preconceived image of the predicted Messiah. The few who did easily recognize Jesus—the magi, Simeon, Anna—did so not because they perfectly understood the old prophecies but because they responded humbly to the old prophecies by continually praying and searching in the present.

Earlier, I told the story of my wife's dream about trees growing in our loft apartment and being transplanted around our city. We perceived the dream was from God. Then, since the Bible sometimes uses trees to represent kingdom ministries, we interpreted the dream to mean that God would start a ministry in our apartment and spread it from there. The next question was: how should we apply it? We decided to start a group Bible study in our home, and it grew into a church that spawned many small groups and eventually other churches. So the dream came true perfectly. However, at the time, Sonya and I weren't sure we knew the way to go. We first wondered if maybe the dream spoke of a music ministry we were thinking about doing. Since we were both incredibly busy, we also wondered if our job wasn't to invite a local ministry into our home rather than starting a new enterprise ourselves. We weren't sure, but God had spoken strongly, so we chose as best we could. Since we felt unsure about what we were doing, we were totally primed to hear God's follow-up direction to prepare the ministry to be handed off to someone else. Our faith led to action; our uncertainty opened us to additional clarification. Prophecies often work best that way.

Delivering prophecies. Part of prophetic ministry involves delivering prophetic words to other people, and, ideally, when we prophesy to someone, we'll not only share what we've perceived and interpreted, but also a bit about how we think the person might put our prophecy into practice. But if we have to be humble when applying prophecies to our own lives, we have to be doubly humble when delivering words for application in others' lives.

If we have to be humble when applying prophecies to our own lives, we have to be doubly humble when delivering words for application in others' lives.

Again, the meaning and application of prophecies often unfold over time. When we're delivering a prophetic word to someone, we might not know in that moment all that the prophecy will mean for the person. So, the key to good delivery is to not pretend to know more than we do.

We'll want to prophesy boldly and accurately to inspire faith, but we want people to understand that we might not know everything and that they may need to seek God for further information. We invite people to trust our revelations but also to work with them. In tone, we want to sound as if we're giving prophetic guidance but not prophetic edicts or commands.

I once prophesied to a stranger, "I have a strong vision of you being stuck in an actual prison, and somehow you're given keys to everyone's cell doors, as if you could set them all free, but you yourself can't leave." I continued, "I'm sorry, sir, you don't strike me as a criminal who will end up in prison, but this was a strong picture! Can you help me understand it?"

The man laughed. It turned out he was an employee at a local prison, and though he disliked his job, he suspected he should stay there and start a ministry to prisoners. God was confirming this. The vision worked out because I was willing to admit I didn't understand all of it.

When I share prophecies for people, I frequently use gentle phrases like *I think* or *it seems to me* because I want to be honest about the possibility that I don't have the interpretation or application quite right. If people understand this, they're able to consider the prophecy for themselves.

Accordingly, it's often helpful for prophetic ministers to give some indication of confidence. If you feel particularly sure or unsure about your grasp of a given prophecy, you can just say so. Experience helps with this. My years of ministry have not only matured my ability to interpret and apply well, they've also helped me develop a sense for the degree to which I've really nailed the meaning of a given prophecy. I can sound very confident when it's warranted, but I can also say, "I'm a bit fuzzy on this one, so take it under advisement."

In the same vein, it's good to respect track records. If some young believer gives me a prophetic word about my life, I consider it, but if a mature minister with a ten-year record of accurate revelations gives me a word, I consider it very much. (Very mature prophetic ministers are a treasure in any church.)

Paul says that prophetic ministry is for people's "strengthening, encouraging and comfort" (1 Corinthians 14:3), so, when I deliver a prophecy, I just ask myself, *What can I do to make sure this person hears the prophecy well and gets the most out of it?* Sometimes this means that I wait a while to share my revelation, or that I ask the person a few questions about his or her life so I know the situation I'm speaking to. Almost always the best choice is to prophesy in a mild and respectful manner. A good prophet thinks like a sensitive shepherd.

Confirmation. One of the reasons I can afford to be gentle about how I share prophecies is because in the age of the Holy Spirit I know

> A good prophet thinks like a sensitive shepherd.

that God can underscore what I say by offering up the very same revelation through other believers. Indeed, as we discussed earlier, the rule of confirmation can be an important check in the process of application. If one person prophesies that I should become a missionary to Uganda, I find it interesting. But if six people independently prophesy that I should go to Uganda, I get moving.

Often when I deliver a prophecy, I tell the recipient to pray about it to see if the Lord will directly confirm it to him or her in some way. I don't insist on immediate acceptance; I merely encourage the active pursuit of confirmation.

The virtue of mistakes. One of the big keys to making prophetic ministry work well in churches and fellowships is to explain to everyone that even accurate revelations often have puzzling interpretations and applications, and so mistakes get made. Though nervous senior pastors might think it's vital to never give an inaccurate prophecy in a public service, the truly vital thing is to acknowledge when inaccurate prophecies are made so that people know the leadership is being honest and responsible in the learning process. In this way mistakes can actually build trust and teach the congregation to help with confirmation and discernment.

We often give "words of knowledge" in our church services: we prophetically call out the names of strangers and maybe hidden medical conditions or other life details that we couldn't know naturally. We commit to being as specific as possible with the details of these revelations so that people will definitely know if the words apply to them and if they are inaccurate. Although even our novices participate, I would say that these little prophecies prove accurate six out of seven times in our church, and they're often stunningly accurate. (Just recently one of our prayer warriors who had been struggling bravely against a mental illness that tempted her to doubt her judgment accurately called out the first name and a hidden medical condition of a visiting stranger, and then proceeded to heal a fourteen-year-long debilitation.) I make a point of publicly reporting when a word has been proven accurate, but I also call out inaccuracies when I have a good opportunity. By doing both, I demonstrate trustworthy authenticity.

Prophecy and evangelism. My favorite way to use prophecy is evangelistically. People at my church have standing orders to bring me any and every visitor we have. I ask the newcomers if I can pray a little blessing over them, and while praying I try to slip in a little prophecy: "Hey, the Lord shows me that you're searching for a job right now, and I think there may be an opportunity for you in a legal office, so I just bless that." Or maybe something simpler: "I sense that you're musically gifted, and I feel that the Lord wants me to pray that you'd experience renewed joy in that area." Our people will often invite nonbelieving friends to services or home groups just so they can experience prophetic ministry. I've seen quite a number of people come to know the Lord this way. As Paul says, "If an unbeliever or inquirer comes in while everyone is prophesying, . . . the secrets of their hearts are laid bare. So they will fall down and worship God, exclaiming, 'God is really among you!'" (1 Corinthians 14:24-25).

Believers can also take prophetic outreach to the streets—like Jesus did when first meeting the Samaritan woman at the well. After engaging her in conversation, he inserted a prophecy: "You've had five husbands, and the man you now have is not your husband" (John 4:18). It was a bit impolite, but it shook her open, and Jesus then honored her by revealing himself as the Messiah.

My friend Nate Bobbit, a great missions pastor, has a knack for prophesying to strangers in strange places. Once, while shopping at Home Depot, he experienced a sudden and acute pain in his left leg, which he interpreted as a sign that someone nearby needed a corresponding healing. After some searching, he finally questioned the cashier at the checkout counter: "Um, you wouldn't happen to have a painful condition in your left leg, would you?" A couple minutes later, the woman was healed of her chronic sciatica.

Of course, delivering a prophecy to nonbelievers can be extra-awkward because they obviously won't be used to such things. You'll usually have to invite them to consider your message rather than presuming they'll accept it. And you'll want to take extraordinary care if your message has to do with a need for repentance from specific sins. (I've only attempted to deliver such prophecies a few times in the past twenty years!) The point is not just to show that the Lord knows, but that the Lord knows and loves.

> The point is not just to show that the Lord knows, but that the Lord knows and loves.

Getting Started: The Practice of Practice

Perceiving revelation requires cultivating awareness; interpreting prophecies requires learning symbolic alphabets; delivering prophecies requires exercising sensitivity. In short, the ministry of prophecy takes a decent amount of practice. You'll probably find your own ways to do things, but here are some of my tried-and-true suggestions for developing the practice of practicing.

First, don't pray without listening. God speaks, so it's impolite to not listen.

Second, practice in small groups. In our church's home groups we typically gather people into a circle, put someone in the center and then have the ring of people prophesy together for the person. We call this the "mushpot" because the person in the middle has the mildly disturbing sensation of being thrown into a pot. But the advantage is that everyone is encouraged to practice listening and to "workshop" interpretations together. It builds prophetic community.

Third, see that novice prophetic ministers hang around more mature ministers during times of prophetic ministry. When the mature minister prophesies, the novice will often say, "Oh, I guess I was sort of sensing that, too, but I didn't realize what it was." It helps train novices to notice.

Fourth, keep a tablet by your bed and write a line or two about your dreams when you wake up. Don't write down whole dreams because it takes too long, and the real point is just to train your mind to recall dreams and their symbols. You can work on discerning whether dreams are prophetic, and you can practice symbolic interpretation. Everyone dreams, so it's a great general exercise.

Fifth, read a ton of Scripture. A large portion of prophetic symbols and signs will be borrowed from the Bible, and it pays to have them tucked away in your head.

Sixth, make sure to act on your prophecies if you can. If it looks really risky, then seek confirmation first. But the best way to improve your prophetic understanding—to determine your hits and misses—

is to try stuff out. The more active your life, the more guidance God will be compelled to give you!

A Prophetic Sort of Life

My life is based on gospel revelation that is centuries old, but my life is often shaped by personal prophecies in the present.

When I wondered what to do after college, the Lord spoke a phrase that led me to move into a violent, impoverished neighborhood and start a ministry. Three years later he suddenly told me to leave the area, so I went to graduate school in Chicago. In grad school he supernaturally directed my wife and me to start a ministry that became a church, and then to leave the city. When we later settled in Boston, the Lord gave me a series of visions about traveling to Cuba (of all places), and when I finally got there I immediately met a young pastor who had seen in a vision that he would be receiving a visitor from Boston. That started an international ministry that continues today in a number of challenging countries. A bit later, the Lord sent words through several people to direct Sonya and me to move to Hawaii, where we ultimately planted a church that is itself working to plant churches in unreached places. Scripture can explain my beliefs, but I can't explain my story without talking about prophecy.

I think this adds a great deal to my life. As I let my life be shaped by personal prophecies, I'm finding my personal path and calling with the Lord. I'm being led personally. I think this way of life releases kingdom daring.

Some people fear that prophetic ministry will be abused by those seeking to manipulate others or draw attention to themselves, and this can happen. But anyone who really embraces prophetic ministry knows that it's hardly a guarantee of perfect foreknowledge or smooth sailing, so when I see my companions live out their prophecies by, say, reaching out to a particular stranger, by making extraordinary material sacrifices or by moving to a needy country, then I see courage, not arrogance. They're living by guidance, not by guarantees. It's both powerful and vulnerable. It's supernatural.

Crazy Connection

When I started to get to know Vern (short for Veronica), I was immediately refreshed by her no-nonsense attitude. I was also impressed that someone so small could down three pints of beer without feeling it. Vern projected an almost impatient desire to help people in trouble, which made her an awesome addition to our community, but she definitely didn't strike me as one of those super-spiritual types. She didn't get teary-eyed during the worship music at church, and she wasn't going to spend hours a day in prayer; there was too much "real work" to do. But then she discovered that spiritual power could be practical, and she dove in head first.

After being with us for just about six months, she walked into my office one afternoon and asked me for all my teaching notes on supernatural ministry. She was planning a trip to see her parents in Delaware and had decided that she was going to conduct a healing seminar at their little church. "I just don't think anyone has ever told them about using the supernatural stuff," she explained. I handed over my notes, she read them on the plane, and, as she later learned, a guy got healed of cancer at that seminar.

Today, Vern leads our justice ministry, which means, among other things, that she runs our outreach and rescue efforts for victims of the sex industry. In any given week the justice outreach team deals with violence, unthinkable emotional deprivations, seedy locales, homelessness, extreme poverty, intense demonic deliverances, narcotics and frustrating legal labyrinths. The team has helped free dozens of women and girls from the industry in the past couple of years. But it all seems quite impossible when you see it up close. Many cases seem hopeless right up until they're not.

"We don't just need to pray," Vern announced during one especially intense season, "we need to pray together daily for the specific situations we're working on. Otherwise I think we're dead."

So a group of our justice ministers started to meet daily for prayer. I don't know how they fit it into their schedules, since most of them, including Vern, hold down jobs in the business world while maintaining staggering ministry commitments. But time and again, when the team needs a breakthrough, their sacrifice leads to uncanny responses to prayer.

Several months ago the team heard through the grapevine that one of the local pimps was leaving the island within a couple days. Normally we like it when pimps leave our island, but this particular pimp was leaving to avoid charges forming against him due to the testimony of an underage girl our team had helped rescue. It takes a tremendous amount of courage for a prostituted woman to testify against her pimp because she faces the double threat of violent retribution from criminals and legal prosecution from authorities. We didn't want this pimp fleeing and leaving our girl hanging.

Vern immediately called her contacts on the police force, but until the formal charges were filed, there was nothing they could do to stop the guy from boarding the plane. She called the prosecutor's office and even airport security, but no one could help.

So, she rallied the team: "Let's just pray that something happens to keep him off that plane!"

A day passed without any news, and then we received word that at the last second the airline had simply refused him boarding. And the thing is, nobody knows why. There was some inexplicable glitch in the system. He was stuck in town long enough for the charges to be filed.

Some weeks later one of the other rescued teens crumpled under the pressure of living straight and announced that she would be returning to the streets to turn tricks as an "independent." She would do it without a pimp, she said, and it would be fine.

So, once again, Vern rallied the team: "Pray that something dramatic changes her mind before she actually does any business."

The girl hit the streets the next night and within minutes was picked up by a guy cruising in a car. But the fellow turned out to be a new pimp in the neighborhood, trying to scoop up independent working girls without protection. He threatened her with violence, and she got so freaked out that she just hopped out of the car and ran. That was the end of her return to the street.

Recently, one of the women who had come out of the trade and been with us for some time had her own crisis of confidence about going straight. To cope, she spent a night haunting her old drug dens.

"Let's pray that her heart would settle," Vern directed the team, "and that God would provide a way for her to grow more confident."

That weekend the woman came to church repentantly, and tearfully begged me to pray that she could feel differently about her life. I did, and during the prayer the Lord led me to prophesy that he would soon give her chances to tell her story to many people. It was an especially poignant prophecy because the woman suffered from intense social anxiety and had spent years unable to speak at all about the abuse she'd suffered.

A few days later, while visiting a homeless shelter, she happened to cross paths with a state congressman on a fact-finding mission. They struck up a conversation, and the congressman invited her to share at a meeting of civic leaders that afternoon. She went and spoke; one thing led to another and a couple days later she was being interviewed about her life on a network affiliate TV news program. Prophecy fulfilled and prayer for confidence answered.

"It's funny," Vern said to me, "but it seems like whenever we pray for something we need for the ministry, we get it. I pray for other stuff with mixed results, but when I pray for this ministry, it's like there's this crazy connection with heaven."

"Well, you've sacrificed a lot for this ministry," I noted.

She continued, "When we first started, we just laid ourselves out there in love. Then we started praying just to survive. Now it seems like everything happens because of the prayers."

"It reminds me of that verse in John," I said. "'Abide in me and let my words abide in you, then ask whatever you wish and it will be granted to you.'"

Vern perked up. "Ah, yes, there you go. I like practical Scripture."

The Ministry of Intercession

For most of this book we've talked about doing ministry directly as opposed to just petitioning God to do it for us. For example, we don't ask God to preach; we take the message he gives us and we preach it. We don't ask God to heal a sick person; we try to use power from God to supernaturally heal the person ourselves. We don't ask God to cast demons out of people; we use the authority God gives us to cast out their demons.

But sometimes there are situations when we have to petition God to intervene himself—maybe because we have no direct access to the situations or because we simply don't know what we can do to help. We don't want to pester God to do ministry he's actually given us to do, but, let's face it, if we're out there trying to change the world, we'll probably need to ask God to intervene directly from time to time.

> If we're out there trying to change the world, we'll probably need to ask God to intervene directly from time to time.

But, as we've discussed before, God strongly prefers to partner with us to get things done. So, even when we're praying for him to do the work, he gives us a significant partnering role to play. To pave the way for God's powerful responses to our prayers, he gives us the ministry to others called intercession.

The ministry of intercession releases power for others through our prayers on their behalf. So, intercession is definitely what you would call a supernatural ministry, and like the other supernatural ministries we've talked about, it can take a lot of work.

Intercession gets a decent amount of attention among believers today, especially among those who are passionate about prayer. But I suspect the ministry is often misunderstood. Many believers seem to think that intercession is simply praying for other people. When they intercede for a person, they mean that they intensely pray that God would bless the person in some certain way. But intercession is more than just praying for others. It's praying for others from a certain spiritual position.

When advising Timothy on how to pray for people, Paul says, "I urge, then, first of all, that requests, prayers, intercessions . . . be made for all people" (1 Timothy 2:1). He suggests that we make requests for people, prayers for people and intercession for people—which means he saw intercession as a distinct activity. The biblical Greek word for intercession, *entynchanō*, comes from a combination of root words meaning something like "through" and "obtain." It suggests the act of obtaining something through an intermediary. An intercessor is a go-between—or, if you will, a representative. When we make intercession to God for people, we don't merely make petitions to God for them; we petition God as their representative.

Being a representative to God presumes that you have a strong, open ministry connection with God. We've already discussed at length how you might pursue that: you cultivate things like obedience, faith and consecration, and you devote yourself to walking closely with him. Being a representative for people requires that you've achieved some meaningful connection with them, and that's a different sort of work.

One part of intercession is indeed praying to the Lord for others. The other part—the part that people often don't think about—is doing the work that makes you an authentic representative of those you pray for.

What sort of work enables us to represent others in the ministry of intercession? In worldly affairs we can become someone's representative through a legal, financial or political arrangement, but in the kingdom of God we can only represent those to whom we're bonded by works of love. And since the currency of love is sacrifice, we represent people we've sacrificed for. The most powerful sacrifices will be those that involve us sharing in the particular, personal suffering of those we are praying for. That is, we can be identified as someone's representative once we somehow assume his or her burdens.

The Lord is full of grace, and he doubtlessly hears and responds in some way to every prayer we lift, but when we pray from a place of intercession, having sacrificed for those we lift in prayer, then the Lord is likely to release more immediate and powerful responses to our petitions. Why? As we've discussed several times in the book, the Lord desires that his demonstrations of power be preceded with authentic acts of love so the world will associate his power with his love. In God's design, acts of love always precede the release of power in ministry. So, in the ministry of intercession we adopt people's burdens as a sacrificial gesture of love so that the Lord can then respond to our prayers without reservation. This is not to say that we make sacrifices so the Lord will hear our prayers (as if he were some pagan god that needed to be appeased), nor is it to suggest that God is a cosmic candy machine into which we must deposit sacrifices in order to get him to do what we want. Indeed, when we pray for people, we already know that God is eager to bless them. So, intercession isn't appeasement; it's partnership. Intercession is the ministry through which we pave the path for the Lord's interventions. We make sacrifices of love so that the God of love can honor them with power. Intercession effectively gives God the excuse he seeks. And it's yet another way we minister with the Lord instead of merely asking him to minister.

That's the conceptual gist of it, anyway. These big theoretical points always boil down to practical questions, and the million-dollar question about the ministry

> Intercession is the ministry through which we pave the path for the Lord's interventions.

of intercession is, how do you actually go about it? What does it really mean to enter into someone's suffering so you can be the person's representative? What's it like to pray as an intercessor?

Let's fill out the picture a bit by looking at what Scripture says about the way sacrificial love translates into powerful prayers. We'll look at how Jesus became our intercessor, and how we're now included in his intercessory mission. Then I'll suggest a few ways to approach intercessory sacrifices and finish with a point or two about how the Holy Spirit sometimes helps us out in intercession.

Love Made Personal, Prayer Made Powerful

Jesus says, "If you abide in me, and my words abide in you, ask whatever you wish, and it will be done for you" (John 15:7 ESV). Whatever we wish? That's quite something. I'd wish for world peace and maybe the annual demise of the New York Yankees. Alas, Jesus says that to have such great petitionary power we have to "abide" in him and let his words "abide" in us. Abiding in Jesus probably means staying strongly connected to him, and having his words abide in us seems like it would have something to do with staying true to his teachings. Jesus pretty much drives this home a few verses later by saying, "If you obey my commandments, you will abide in my love" (John 15:10 ESV). We might paraphrase the promise by saying, "If you stick close to me and do what I teach, then you can ask whatever you wish and God will give it to you." And that still sounds like a heck of a deal. But it raises the question, what did Jesus teach?

Jesus taught a fair number of things, and much of what he taught was based on ancient Scriptures, which makes for a lot of material. But thankfully he summed it all up for us. Jesus said, "'Love the Lord your God with all your heart and with all your soul and with all your mind.' This is the first and greatest commandment. And the second is like it: 'Love your neighbor as yourself.' All the Law and the Prophets hang on these two commandments" (Matthew 22:37-40). We're taught to love God without reservation—with all our heart, soul and mind—and to love others in such a way as to identify with them—loving them "as yourself."

Jesus essentially tells us that if we love very well, our prayers work very well. John picked up this love-and-prayer theme in his first epistle: We "receive from him anything we ask, because we obey his commands and do what pleases him. And this is his command: to trust in the name of his Son, Jesus Christ, and to love one another as he commanded us" (1 John 3:22-23).

If love is the trigger that releases God's most powerful responses to prayer, then it makes sense that praying most effectively for others will involve us loving them well. We should love people intensely for the sake of praying for them effectively. This is basically what intercession is all about, and if you can't immediately envision what it might look like, no worries. We have an excellent model: Jesus.

We often think of Jesus' legacy in terms of atonement, but his ongoing ministry is actually intercession. Jesus "is able to save completely those who come to God through him, because he always lives to intercede for them" (Hebrews 7:25). We're told that Jesus sits at the Father's right hand and intercedes for us constantly (Romans 8:34), and it's because of Jesus' go-between position that the power of the Holy Spirit was released to us (Acts 2:33).

So, what did Jesus do to become our intercessor? Well, not surprisingly, he loved us. But he didn't just love us; he sacrificed for us. And he didn't just sacrifice for us; he sacrificed by adopting our sorts of suffering.

> We often think of Jesus' legacy in terms of atonement, but his ongoing ministry is actually intercession.

As an atoning sacrifice Jesus merely had to live a short while and die, like a lamb on an altar. But that's not what he did. Instead, he lived with us deeply, shared our every human burden, faced our every temptation and challenge. Why? Because his mission wasn't just to die as an atonement but to enter our suffering in order to become representative. God loved us perfectly before Jesus ever came, but after Jesus' incarnation he could love us as himself (literally). Our suffering became his suffering. He could identify with us and be identified with us. He didn't just die for us; he bonded with us.

I suppose God could have loved us from afar, could have hatched a plan to transform us into his image from a distance, but instead he adopted our image. As if dying for us were not enough, he stands with us as well. I find this a bit difficult to wrap my head around. I think it says that his love is not just great but also personal, accepting and humble. It makes a fuller statement of his heart, and in any case, it's the statement he chooses to make and the one he wants us to demonstrate to the world. He wants us to show a love that doesn't just break barriers but also assumes burdens.

Paul wrote to the Colossians, "Now I rejoice in what I am suffering for you, and I fill up in my flesh what is still lacking in regard to Christ's afflictions, for the sake of his body, which is the church" (Colossians 1:24). Some might be shocked to hear Paul say that something is "still lacking" in Jesus' afflictions, as if his death on the cross were somehow inadequate. But Paul isn't talking about Jesus' role as an atoning sacrifice; he's talking about Jesus' suffering as an intercessor. When Jesus walked the earth, he bonded sacrificially with many people in many situations, and now we get to join in that ministry. The message is: every person is worth suffering for personally. If we put the message into action, our prayers will become extraordinarily powerful.

The Ministry of Sacrifice and Suffering

All ministries are sacrificial, but intercession is a ministry that's specifically about sacrifice and suffering. Sound fun? Well, maybe not in the moment, but it creates fruitfulness, and that will be gratifying when you see it.

When I say that intercession is a ministry of sacrifice and suffering, I mean that, practically speaking, it's a ministry that is largely about finding and applying ways to sacrifice and suffer for people. I know that might sound strange, but I think it's accurate. It usually works something like the following.

First, you encounter people in a situation that requires help from the Lord. If you're like me, you might immediately lift some prayers. "O God, have mercy! Help them in their distress!" You might pray for guidance about how you could help them directly, or you might pray for the Lord to raise up other ministers to help them. But ultimately you decide that you're going to intercede for them so that the Lord might intervene freely and powerfully.

Intercession requires that you somehow enter into their suffering so you can represent them before the Lord. So you ask yourself, *What can I do to suffer with them?* You have to come up with a mode of action. The Lord might inspire you, or you might just hit upon something. And then you have to do it. The ministry consists in the *doing* of sacrificial suffering.

Then, once you're experiencing their burdens somehow, you begin to petition God for help. But now you're not just praying; you're interceding.

To serve as an intercessor we somehow have to make our attachments palpable instead of just conceptual. We have to put our life where our love is. Jesus did it by putting on flesh and walking the earth as a beggar. We might do it by moving to the troubled neighborhood we're praying for, or to the country that we'd like to see blessed. To become an intercessor for broken families, we might adopt children who need homes. To become an intercessor for the poor, we might give away our wealth and live in simplicity. Conversely, it's hard to represent the unreached if we've never sacrificed to reach them, and it would probably be pretty difficult to represent the destitute if we live in a mansion and drive a luxury car. We might love them in our heart, but to put ourselves in a position to intercede, we have to find a way to make a manifest bond of sacrificial love. We don't just ask God to help people with their suffering; we join in the people's suffering and then ask God to help all of us with it.

Obviously, the way we go about doing this will vary from person to person and from situation to situation. Sometimes, we'll see obvious and straightforward ways to connect sacrificially to someone. Other times, we might need to be creative. I've found that the Spirit often guides eager intercessors to specific ideas. But generally, those ideas are going to fall into two general categories worth bearing in mind: situational sacrifices and sympathetic sacrifices.

Situational Sacrifice

What I call situational sacrifice is the simplest and most direct way to achieve an intercessory position for someone. It's when a believer willingly and sacrificially enters into a person's actual situation. For example, the missionary who moves to a famine-plagued, war-torn country to live among the people is clearly adopting the burdens of those he or she seeks to bless. Since the missionary is exposed to the deprivations and dangers of the people, he or she seriously owns their challenges and therefore is in an excellent position to represent them before the Lord.

Earlier, I shared about my friend Vern who has built a ministry for victims of the sex trade in our city. Vern has opened her home as safe lodging for numerous young women (and their newborn babies), has exposed herself to danger from pimps, and has extravagantly shared her time and income. She has blurred the boundaries between her life and the women's lives. Her situation is their situation. As a result of this intercessory lifestyle, it's uncanny how God consistently and creatively answers ministry-related prayers for Vern and her team.

Again, the best biblical example of this sort of intercessory connection is Jesus' incarnation. Through Jesus' birth, God entered into our lowly estate and shared in the deprivations and dangers that go with it—to the point of corporeal suffering and death. Following Jesus' model, believers sometimes talk about doing incarnational ministry—by which they mean ministry that involves adopting the modes and conditions of the lives of those they wish to minister to. The apostle Paul said, "To the Jews I became like a Jew, to win the Jews. To those under the law I became like one under the law, . . . so as to win those under the law. . . . To the weak I became weak, to win the weak. I have become all things to all people so that by all possible means I might save some" (1 Corinthians 9:20, 22). An incarnational approach is sometimes a good way to win people's trust and understanding, but if it's done with sacrifice, it's also a great way to achieve a position of intercessory representation for those people.

A couple years back, two of my good friends from church, John and Andy, were thinking about incarnational intercession while ministering to the homeless population in a rough corner of our city. They decided to forge a bond with the homeless by living on the streets without money or supplies for a while. They came back from the sojourn on the streets with disturbing stories and significantly shrunken waistlines, but I think the exercise added power to their prayers and opened the way for the Lord to move in a new way in our church. Since that time we've never failed to have homeless people participating fruitfully in our congregation.

John and Andy were never truly homeless during their time on the streets because they could choose to return to their normal lifestyle at any time, but the experience was severe enough to be bonding. Indeed, John continues his intercession today by leading our community house ministry. He and other volunteers regularly spend time out on the streets and then invite homeless friends to move home with them as roommates. Many of our church's best supernatural stories come from our outreach to the homeless.

Sympathetic Sacrifice

Sympathetic sacrifice is when a believer forges an experience of solidarity with a person that doesn't involve entering into the person's actual situation. For example, if you want to intercede for a community suffering from AIDS, you can't actually enter into AIDS itself. You can, however, fast from food, offer sleepless vigils, open your home to hospice care or do any number of other things that exercise your willingness to participate in deprivation on account of the situation. Although you're not directly experiencing the challenge, you're sacrificing in sympathy to it and therefore exercising a real bond. You don't share the precise burden, but you share the experience of being burdened.

To some, sympathetic sacrifices might seem like artificial suffering, and they might wonder if God would truly want it. It's one thing to join in a person's challenge, but why add new sorts of suffering? Isn't that psychologically unhealthy? Actually, I think it would be psychologically unhealthy to make yourself miserable for someone if you were doing it out of guilt or because you felt as if you had something to prove, but to make sacrifices of solidarity because you believe it could help empower ministry is an entirely different thing. It's just a way of manifesting a bond of love—the giving of a sacrificial gift so as to say, "I'm with you. I own this too."

The Bible is full of examples of people making sympathetic sacrifices for others. Before Esther risked her life by petitioning King Xerxes for Israel's deliverance, she instructed her people to fast for three days in solidarity with her (Esther 4:16). Similarly, before Ezra and the exiles set out on their journey to rebuild Jerusalem, he directed all the people to fast as a way to intercede with God for safe travels for the travelers and their children (Ezra 8:21-22). When Nehemiah heard of the desolation of Jerusalem, he fasted for three days before petitioning the Lord to grant him favor with King Artaxerxes and to help the Jews to restore the city (Nehemiah 1). Daniel understood through prophetic Scriptures that God planned to restore Israel's exiles to Jerusalem, and yet he still put himself through a season of fasting in sackcloth and ashes, and intensely petitioned the Lord to accomplish the restoration (Daniel 9). The prophet Anna spent decades worshiping in the temple courts, "night and day, fasting and praying" for her nation, until she finally beheld the baby Jesus and proclaimed him the Redeemer (Luke 2:36-38). All these people petitioned the Lord for help, but first they sacrificed in sympathy for the people they wanted to see helped.

When I have occasion to make sympathetic sacrifices, I find it helpful to think along the lines of fasting-in-kind. That is, I often try to tune my fast or sacrifice in a way that somehow reflects the suffering or challenges of the people for whom I want to intercede. For instance, as I mentioned in an earlier chapter, during a fast for cancer sufferers, some friends of mine shaved their heads as part of their intercession for those suffering from the effects of chemotherapy and radiation treatments.

Some other friends, greatly concerned about political oppression and poverty in certain parts of the world, launched a "justice lifestyle" fast in which they sacrificially and carefully chose their food, clothing, energy usage and other consumables in a manner sensitive to the exploitive economics in some developing countries. They wanted to share the sort of material burden that would come with economic and political reform in those places.

My good friends Thomas and Colleen Kuehn are ministers in southern Asia. In hopes of seeing a move of God in that region, they walked across Sri Lanka carrying a large wooden cross. This intercessory act symbolized the carrying of the gospel to the people, and it was sacrificial not only in terms of the physical exertion it required but in the risk to life and limb it posed in a country where many are actively hostile to Jesus followers.

All these are examples of people choosing a sacrifice that somehow matched the situation they were interceding for. The in-kind nature of the sacrifice actually generates sympathetic reactions and emotions within us—we truly feel bits of what it's like to experience the suffering of the people we're interceding for—and this helps foster deeper personal attachment to those people. This attachment, this love, makes our prayers more powerful.

Interceding with the Holy Spirit

The essence of intercession is to share someone's burden and then to pray powerfully to God from that place of burden. We can share the burden situationally or sympathetically. And it turns out that, on occasion, we can share it supernaturally too. This has to do with a certain manifestation of the Holy Spirit within us, and it's a way for the Spirit to include us in his intercession, or perhaps help us to intercede for people we should attend to but haven't yet. It sounds a bit mystical, but it can be extraordinarily helpful.

The Spirit is an intercessor, just as he is a healer, a teacher and revealer. And just as the Spirit helps us with these other ministries, he can lead us in intercession. Paul encouraged his disciples, "In all prayer and intercession, pray always in [or with] the Spirit, and in this way intercede for all the saints" (Ephesians 6:18, my translation). He told the Romans, "the Spirit takes a share in our weakness"— which sounds exactly like an intercessory burden. "We don't know what to pray, but the Spirit himself intercedes for [or with] us with inexpressible groans" (Romans 8:26, my translation). But while Jesus intercedes for people from his place at the Father's throne, the Holy Spirit can intercede for people from within us (Ephesians 2:22). When that happens, we'll sometimes sense it, often intensely.

Believers sometimes speak of "feeling burdened" by the Lord to pray for this or that person or situation. This can be a metaphorical expression, but these burdens can also have a palpable quality. In the same way we might feel the sensation of power flowing through us during a supernatural healing (Mark 5:30), experience spiritual speech articulated in our mouths when speaking in tongues (1 Corinthians 14:2) or have sensory experiences during a prophetic revelation, the Spirit can give us a sense of deep emotional burden, or even physical sensations of travail, in what is essentially an impartation of intercessory suffering. We're given a burden supernaturally, and the point is to then take it to prayer to complete the intercession. It seems to me that the Spirit often works this way to get us moving in the right intercessory direction. As Paul says, often "we don't know what to pray, but the Spirit intercedes" (Romans 8:26, my translation). It's a help to us when we're ignorant of situations that should be benefiting from intercessory ministry. In fact, some people use the term *prophetic intercession* to describe this sort of imparted experience because it reveals the Spirit's intercessory agenda. My friend Jeannie, who helps lead our prayer and intercession teams at church, sometimes finds herself bursting into tears as she starts to pray, and she then has to figure out why the Spirit has her crying. Her sudden sensations of grief or loss eventually lead her to discover situations around her for which she needs to pursue some intercession. Once, while reading quietly, I was overcome with a sense of threat to my friend Paul. After an intense twenty minutes of prayer I got a phone call saying that he'd been in a bad car accident but somehow escaped all injury. It's as if the Spirit shared with me an acute and temporary bond with Paul so that I could pray effectively for God's intervention at the time of crisis. It all seems strange unless you appreciate just how serious the Lord is about partnering with us for the release of his power in the world. Normally, we partner with him through hard work and sacrifice, but he's not above a little sovereign impartation from time to time in special situations. You could call it a gift of intercession.

In any case, if you sense the Spirit's intercessory burdens within you, you should pray into them, or as Paul says, "pray [with] the Spirit and in this way intercede." Hopefully, you'll already have a strong, prayerful relationship with the Father. Your devotion will make you a ready conduit for the work of the Spirit in this way. And hopefully whatever episodes of supernatural burdens you experience will fortify you for other forms of sacrificial suffering.

Living as an Intercessor

To make intercession means to bond with people through acts of loving sacrifice so that we can represent the people before the Lord in prayer and release powerful interventions from God. We don't sacrifice because God needs to be appeased but because God has great reason to want demonstrations of love to accompany breakthroughs of his power. Intercession paves the way for God's responses. It's the way we partner with God to bring his interventions in the world.

> Intercession is the way we partner with God to bring his interventions in the world.

The ministry of intercession typifies the sort of lifestyle we're called to lead as followers of Jesus—or maybe it's that the kingdom life amplifies intercession. You could put it both ways. Our kingdom calling, in a nutshell, is to bring the love of God to people and to bring people to the God of love. We're supposed to be a bridge of sorts. We connect strongly to God with one hand and strongly to people with the other. When we do it precisely to empower prayerful petitions, we call it the ministry of intercession, but when we do it generally to spread the kingdom and its message, we just call it gospel living. One way or another, experienced believers always try to be bridge builders, loving sacrificers, burden sharers and power bringers.

And just as the ministry of intercession is such a clear complement to kingdom living, it will be a powerful complement to other kingdom ministries we do. When there's no way for us to accomplish what we need through direct ministry, we can intercede for God's interventions. But after God intervenes in situations, we usually find it creates new opportunities for us to minister directly. This is always a great thing to ask for when we make intercession for people. We ask the Lord to provide the breakthroughs that will open up the harvest, and then to raise us up to work the harvest well.

The Spirit, Baby

About eight years ago I was offered a ministry job at a Presbyterian church in Honolulu. I'd spent my adult life ministering in "Spirit-filled" churches, and at the time I was doing some missions work in a politically oppressed country, so it was hard for me to imagine transitioning to a buttoned-down, mainline church with no history of supernatural ministry. But oddly enough, God seemed to be in it, and the senior pastor said he'd consider me a "missionary to the Presbyterians." Thus began an interesting and educational sojourn.

Mostly I found that my Presbyterian family didn't have theological objections to the way I worked and lived, but I did have to deal with certain barriers of custom. Sometimes what believers think about the supernatural power of God isn't nearly as restrictive as the plain fact that they're used to doing things without bothering with the supernatural. So I thought a lot about how to introduce supernatural ministry to perfectly sincere believers who'd simply been conditioned to ignore it.

Eventually I got the idea for a Holy Spirit retreat. From the earliest days of the faith, new believers have been introduced to God's supernatural power through what Scripture calls "the baptism of the Holy Spirit." Typically, ministers lay hands on new believers and the Lord sends the Holy Spirit to baptize or douse them. This baptism usually comes with some obvious supernatural manifestation—recipients might spontaneously speak in tongues or prophesy. More generally, they "receive power" to become "witnesses" (Acts 1:8). This was an introductory experience for new believers in the early church, but today many church traditions have lost the practice entirely.

My idea was to take some believers on a weekend retreat to study the baptism of the Holy Spirit in Scripture, and then to lay hands on them that they might receive it. I hoped for a combination of education and real experience.

Part of my job at my new church was to do outreach to young people, and I'd gathered a group of mostly twenty-somethings who became my guinea pigs for this venture. The group included a couple of military officers, a former exotic dancer, a cult abuse victim, a brain-injured car-crash victim, some depressed grad students, an unemployed grad school dropout, a real estate speculator, and a single mom and her two kids. Fully half of them were under the care of a physician for some kind of mental or emotional illness. We had some Caucasians, some Asians and some Polynesians. A good number of them were new believers. Few of them had any discipleship experience and almost none had ever tried any sort of ministry. They were perfect.

I went with about fifteen of them to a campground on Oahu's north shore, and we studied every passage in the Bible on the baptism of the Spirit. Then, to keep it real, we had a campfire time of confessing our sins (only the embarrassing ones) and pronouncing forgiveness. It was liberating.

Finally, on Saturday night I had everyone gather on the beach near the surf for the time of praying and laying on hands. And, I must say, this is where I showed my genius. The reason I had the prayer time near the surf was because I expected at least some of them to receive the gift of tongues as the Spirit filled them, and the white noise of the tumbling water would keep them from being self-conscious about speaking out. I'm telling you, it was brilliantly sensitive.

But as we gathered, my friend Rachal explained to me that her husband, Will, had a phobia about waves.

"I don't think he should be close to the water," she said.

"Can I just stand up the hill a ways?" asked Will.

Another guy, Kevin, interrupted, "This sand is getting in my pant cuffs! Ugh, I hate that. I should have worn shorts. Wait, I'm going to go get my shorts!"

Dawn, our well-tanned fitness buff, interjected, "Mosquitoes! Mosquitoes, everyone! We've got to do this back at the cabin!"

"Everybody just shut up and get in a circle," I yelled—with brilliant sensitivity.

And then, when people finally quieted, I stood in the middle of the circle and asked God to send us his Holy Spirit.

And we waited.

Over the years I've gotten to administer the baptism of the Holy Spirit so many times that I couldn't begin to count them. But there's always this moment—the moment when we're just waiting for God. It's a conditional moment: either God does something manifestly supernatural or I look silly and everyone feels let down. I'm at a place now where I almost savor this moment of delay, just as one might appreciate the hungry minutes spent enjoying the aroma of a fine dinner before it's actually brought from the kitchen and served. But honestly, on that night my approach was so new, and the support for my attempt so tentative, that I felt a little pressure. I could only guess what my young friends were thinking.

Months later one of the participants of that night confessed to me,

"I felt like a complete moron just standing there like we were waiting for Santa. Then I looked at you, standing in the middle with your hands up, calling for God, and I thought, *No, that guy's the moron*."

Of course, the Spirit moved. He came quietly at first, and I could see him manifest on people as they started to shake softly, then more strongly, with the power that flowed into their bodies.

My friend Kevin, with his cuffs carefully rolled up, was knocked unconscious by the power of the Spirit and took a headlong face plant into the sand, where he stayed a good while. Dawn sang out loudly in tongues. Rachal shivered electrically and wept as she spoke softly in her new tongues. Will felt compelled by the Spirit to throw himself into the waves. He walked into the water and knelt in the surf with his arms opened wide.

Ed, a 365-pound Tongan, filled quickly with power and erupted in new tongues. His eyes got as big as saucers and he pumped his fists in triumph. "I'm speaking in tongues, baby!" he screamed. "The Spirit, baby, yeah!"

He leaped like a dancer, then rolled himself into the water, then hopped up again, splashing, then sprinting, all the while whooping at the top of his lungs, "Tongues, baby!" Tongans know how to celebrate. I watched him plowing along the surf line until he disappeared into the darkness about fifty yards down the sand, his shouts provoking a number of searching flashlights from alarmed campers on the other end of the beach. Again, brilliantly sensitive.

I watched as the Spirit started to touch Ashleigh, a wonderfully intelligent Army lieutenant who had joined us that night out of loyalty, not expectation. Ashleigh was probably the most natural minister in the group. She was the child of missionary parents and knew a thing or two about religious experience. But she did not go in for the supernatural stuff. Long afterward she would explain to me, "I was there because my friends had decided to go, but I told myself there was no way I was going to let anything weird happen. I mean, nothing could happen, right?"

As she quivered visibly in the Spirit's power, I sensed prophetically—I could almost see with my eyes—that there was a spiritual blockage of sorts in her, and I pointed to the center of her chest and said, "It's a fear, and it's stuck right here." She opened her eyes, looked at me tearfully and nodded firmly.

"Now it's moving," I said, and raised my pointing finger upward from her chest to her throat, and finally to her quivering mouth, at which point she immediately burst out in fluent tongues, her lips struggling to keep up with her words, and she was filled to brimming with the power of the Holy Spirit.

It was a night full of change for our motley crew. From that small group of people, we launched a supernatural outreach service that drew in others. When my time with the brave Presbyterian church was over, the remnants and descendants of the group planted a new church, which has drawn in yet more and launched new missionary ventures around the globe. The handful of individuals in that original small group would go on to conduct Holy Spirit retreats across Hawaii, the US mainland and at least five other countries.

Five years after that first retreat, Ashleigh received transfer orders from the Army, and some of the original gang gathered together to reminisce before she left.

"Yeah, that Holy Spirit retreat on the beach," she said, "totally not what I had in mind. But it seemed like everything sort of started there."

"What exactly would you say happened there?" I asked.

"Well, God showed up, didn't he?" Ashleigh has a way of rounding off her conclusions with a question. "Maybe that's all it was. You don't expect anything, and then God shows up, and then everything's different, isn't it?"

The Baptism of the Holy Spirit

In the biblical accounts of the early church, the baptism of the Holy Spirit is a big deal. When Jesus last spoke to his disciples, he told them, "Do not leave Jerusalem, but wait for the gift my Father promised, which you have heard me speak about. For John baptized with water, but in a few days you will be baptized with the Holy Spirit" (Act 1:4-5). At the end of Luke's Gospel, Jesus' final instructions are recorded even more bluntly: "I am going to send you what my Father has promised, but stay in the city until you have been clothed with power from on high" (Luke 24:49). Jesus ordered his disciples to not start their mission until the baptism of the Spirit had come to them. He made it sound essential.

At the time, the disciples probably had no idea what Jesus was talking about, but about ten days later, something happened. A bunch of followers were together praying when suddenly they heard "a sound like the blowing of a violent wind," and "tongues of fire" appeared in the air and came to rest on each of them, and they "began to speak in other tongues as the Spirit enabled them" (Acts 2:1-4).

Well, this was new.

I imagine it was also a little freaky at first. We're not given details of how the experience affected the disciples physically, but when they finally spilled out onto the streets, onlookers said they seemed drunk, so they might have been a little woozy or shockingly unrestrained. The onlookers were also astonished that the rough group of Galilean disciples had suddenly developed the capacity to speak in so many different tongues. It caused quite a big scene, and Peter took advantage of the excitement by standing tall and preaching his first big sermon.

He judiciously explained that the disciples weren't drunk. Then he said,

> This is what was spoken by the prophet Joel:
>
> "In the last days, God says,
> I will pour out my Spirit on all people." (Acts 2:16-17)

The Holy Spirit had only made cameo appearances in the Old Testament, filling only a handful of individuals with special power at various times. But now all believers had access to the filling all the time. Peter understood this momentous change, and he understood it had been foreseen by God's prophet over six centuries earlier. At the end of Peter's impromptu street sermon, three thousand people "accepted his message and were baptized."

That's how it all started for the church. That was the beginning of Christian outreach. And given the historical role of the baptism of the Holy Spirit and the value given it by Jesus and his disciples, it's astonishing that so many churches no longer pursue it at all.

Since the Spirit's baptism marked the beginning of the church's ministry, and since Scripture suggests it should be one of the early steps in our individual walk with Jesus, you might think I'd put my discussion of it at the beginning of this book instead of toward the end. You know, first things first. But by delaying it until now, I'm hoping it will be easier to explain what it's for and why it happens as it does. Unfortunately, explaining the Spirit's baptism is sometimes complicated by the substantial amount of controversy it's generated among churches. Most of it is anchored in theological and political squabbles dating to the Pentecostal revivals of the early twentieth century, and almost all of it is avoidable because what Scripture says about the Spirit's baptism is really quite accessible.

In fact, depending on how you slice them up, there are only about fifty verses that directly concern the baptism of the Spirit, and twenty-one of them are in the story of Pentecost in Acts 2. Here's a decent reference list: Matthew 3:11; Mark 1:8; Luke 3:16; John 1:33; Acts 1:8; 2:1-21, 38; 4:29-31; 8:14-24; 10:44-46; 15:8; 19:1-7. If you want to be more loosely inclusive, you might add Luke 11:11-13 (in which Jesus declares the Father is eager to "give the Holy Spirit to those who ask him") and John 14:26; 16:7 (in which Jesus explains the Holy Spirit will be sent to help us). You could print all the essential Scriptures on a couple notebook pages, and when you read them all together you'd find that there's little in the way of complicated theology there. Mostly you'll find straightforward descriptions of people's experiences with the baptism. You might think it would be easy to come up with a decent working understanding—a plain and powerful instructional teaching on baptism of the Spirit.

So, here goes.

I'll try to work through the issues that sometimes make the baptism of the Spirit seem complicated to people, and then we'll tackle the practical issues of administering and receiving it. I think we can do this by asking five basic questions: What is the baptism of the Holy Spirit and what is it for? What can we expect to happen during a Holy Spirit baptism? How can we be sure we've received the baptism of the Spirit? (It's a trick question, because the point isn't whether we've received "it" but whether we want more.) Who gets the baptism of the Holy Spirit? And how do we go about getting the baptism of the Holy Spirit?

What Is the Baptism of the Holy Spirit?

Here's the essential cheat sheet on the baptism of the Holy Spirit: The baptism of the Spirit is an empowering manifestation of God's indwelling presence in an individual. The baptism involves the Spirit manifesting in an individual with such intensity that supernatural things tend to occur in that moment—most notably the expression of spiritual gifts such as tongues or prophecy—and the power that adheres in the person as a result helps him or her live and minister supernaturally, which is the real goal. Believers typically don't receive the baptism of the Spirit until they attend to it directly, and having received it they can certainly seek repeated dousings of the Spirit's presence and power. We can receive the baptism through the administration of other believers—typically with the laying on of hands—which means that the baptism of the Spirit should be an active ministry in our churches and fellowships.

There. You could take all that as a nice, working definition, I think.

But a definition is not necessarily an explanation, and the baptism of the Spirit is

> The baptism of the Spirit is an empowering manifestation of God's indwelling presence in an individual.

one of those things that often need a little explaining. Even inexperienced believers will have an intuitive understanding of things like healings, deliverances and prophecies, but many believers have no idea what the baptism of the Spirit is, in part because it may never have even been addressed in their circles, and in part because there's really nothing similar to compare it to. It's a very different sort of experience, and it always has been.

For example, in Acts 8 we read about Simon, a Samaritan sorcerer who, historians tells us, was quite famous. Simon was greatly impressed when he saw Philip's supernatural healings and deliverances in Samaria, but when he then saw Peter and John administer the baptism of the Spirit to people, he was absolutely enthralled. He even offered them money if they would give him the ability. As a professional "supernaturalist," Simon recognized it as something entirely unique.

That might be a good way to approach the Spirit's baptism: it is what it is, and it's not anything else.

For instance, it's often helpful to reassure people that the baptism of the Spirit is not about our basic salvation. A few radical thinkers from the early Pentecostal movement suggested that believers needed to have a definite Spirit baptism experience in order to be truly saved. Jesus, for his part, saw it quite differently. He didn't say that the baptism qualified you to be a follower; he said it empowered you to be a great witness.

"You will be baptized with the Holy Spirit," Jesus said, and "you will receive power when the Holy Spirit comes on you; and you will be my witnesses in Jerusalem, and in all Judea and Samaria, and to the ends of the earth" (Acts 1:5, 8). The baptism of the Spirit brings us supernatural power for witnessing—in whatever way we need it. Sometimes we need miraculous power for healings or deliverances (Acts 8:4-8), and sometimes we just need supernatural help in being bold (Acts 4:29-31). Whatever the application, the baptism of the Spirit is an essential way to "receive power" or, as Jesus put it, to be "clothed with power from on high" (Luke 24:49).

It's not a salvation thing. It's a power thing.

This empowering is a matter of degrees, but on a significant scale. The Greek word in Scripture we usually translate "baptism" literally means "dousing" or "soaking." The disciples had experienced a lot of the Holy Spirit in the years they spent ministering with Jesus, but then Jesus told them they would soon be doused in the Holy Spirit—as if, until then, they had only been dampened. The very term suggests a great increase in intensity. It's not as if the Holy Spirit isn't always active in the life of every believer (he is!), and it's not as if we can't do lots of different things to develop in God's supernatural power (for instance, we've discussed ways to grow in authority, gifting, faith and consecration for power), but when we receive the dousing of the Spirit, we get a windfall increase of his presence and power in us. The baptism of the Spirit is essentially a big supernatural boost.

The word *boost* isn't a glamorous one, but I think it's a good one because it suggests a surge in magnitude. If you'll pardon the analogy, it's a little like the "power boost" features found in a lot of video games. When a video game race car comes upon the special golden fuel can (I'm thinking of a game my son plays), it can suddenly accelerate to jet speed. It's not that the car didn't have power before; it's just that it now has five times as much. To get doused in the Spirit is to have way more of the Spirit's presence and power than before.

We might also say that the baptism of the Spirit works a little like spiritual gifts do. You'll remember from previous discussions that spiritual gifts are essentially God's way of giving each of us a little boost in specific ministry areas. For example, any believer can heal a sick person, but a believer who has the gift of healing will have a much easier time healing people. Well, the baptism of the Spirit is like a spiritual gift except that it brings a supernatural boost across the board—in everything we do. This is because the baptism of the Holy Spirit isn't just an impartation of ability; it's an impartation of God's very presence, which is the source of all power. When we receive the baptism, we receive a surge of God's indwelling Spirit, which then brings us a surge of supernatural power.

The baptism of the Holy Spirit isn't just an impartation of ability; it's an impartation of God's very presence.

It might seem confusing to talk about a "surge" of God's presence, because we believe that God is omnipresent. He's everywhere at all times. How can we talk of receiving his presence if he's already present everywhere?

Well, God is omnipresent, but he manifests his presence in different ways. For instance, though God is everywhere, Jesus walked the earth as a localized, flesh-wrapped manifestation of God's presence. So, too, God's Spirit is everywhere, but the Spirit manifests locally, in space and time, in specific ways. This is why Jesus could speak of the Spirit's "coming," and why he could say the Spirit "lives with you and will be in you" (John 14:17-18). God is everywhere, but he expresses himself manifestly—materially, experientially—in specific modes and locations.

I think believers have always had a decent understanding of this. For example, in the Old Testament it was often said that the Spirit of God "fell upon" this or that person. In the same way, Jesus said that the Holy Spirit would "come upon" the disciples and give them power from on high.

So, to summarize, the baptism of the Holy Spirit is a personal dousing of the Spirit's manifest presence that results in a profound boost of supernatural power in our lives and ministry.

But since we're dealing with a manifestation of God's very presence, we have to mention not just function but also character. The Spirit doesn't just bring power; he brings power with a father's love. Jesus appreciated this deeply. When the Spirit came upon Jesus at his water baptism, a voice from heaven said, "This is my beloved Son, in whom I am well pleased" (Matthew 3:17 KJV). And when Jesus spoke to the disciples in John 14 of the coming of the Spirit, he said, "I will not leave you as orphans" (v. 18). God's Spirit of power is also a Spirit of adoption, and the baptism of the Spirit brings power with intimacy and affirmation. You'll notice that those who experience the baptism are at least as likely to describe it in terms of God's love as God's power. As I've said often, they go together.

What Happens During the Baptism of the Spirit?

When we get doused in the Spirit, we experience God's manifest presence and his supernatural power, and if the all-powerful God manifests in us, there will probably be accompanying evidence. The whole idea of a dousing is that it's relatively extreme, so, one way or another, there will be some indication that it's happened.

But exactly what that indication is can vary a great deal—because each person is different, because God is relational and individually focused, and because the Lord is wonderfully creative.

For instance, when the Spirit first doused the disciples in Acts 2, we read about a curious manifestation of "what seemed to be tongues of fire that separated and came to rest on each of them" (v. 3). This particular manifestation is never again mentioned in any of the biblical accounts of Holy Spirit baptisms. The Spirit came in Acts 2 with "the sound of a mighty wind," but this too only happens once. In Acts 4, when the Spirit falls with power, the building is shaken, but that only happens the one time in Scripture. When the Spirit came upon Jesus at his baptism (Luke 3:21-22), a voice from heaven spoke and a dovelike apparition appeared, but those things were unique to Jesus' experience. In Acts 2, 10 and 19 the dousing of the Spirit manifests with the speaking of tongues. In Acts 4 and 8 the dousing is described without mention of tongues. In Acts 19 the Ephesian believers who experienced the baptism of the Spirit began prophesying, but this specific manifestation isn't mentioned elsewhere.

In my experience of receiving and administering the baptism of the Spirit, I've seen an impressive range of manifestations. Often, people have a profound emotional reaction to God's presence (as one might well expect!), so it's common to see people weep or laugh or spontaneously celebrate when they sense the Spirit come upon them. I also frequently see generic physical manifestations as people's bodies react to the outpouring of power in them. It's common for people to quiver, faint, get a little woozy or simply feel sensations of heat or tingling. It's also very common to see spiritual gifts emerge dramatically when the Spirit comes with power, which makes sense: spiritual gifts are an expression of God's power in us, so it stands to reason that a dousing of God's power would often express itself in a manifestation of these gifts. People most often associate Holy Spirit baptisms with the gift of tongues, but it's not uncommon for people alternately to receive, say, visions or prophetic utterances in an obvious way. All sorts of spiritual gifts can be imparted or empowered during Holy Spirit baptisms, but not all of them are immediately evident. For example, a person might experience a lot of heat in his or her hands during a baptism, but we won't really know if that's a sign of the gift of healing until the person starts laying hands on sick people.

So we can expect the dousing of the Spirit to come with a wide variety of manifestations, some of which are reactions to God's presence and power (emotional expressions, physical sensations) and some of which are the specific products of God's presence and power (boldness, spiritual gifts). A person who receives the dousing of the Spirit can expect something to happen, though the exact experience will be hard to predict, and a good guideline is to just try to be open to whatever the Spirit brings.

Some Christians claim that speaking in tongues is the only true evidence of the baptism of the Spirit: if you don't speak in tongues, you haven't been doused with the Spirit, or so the thinking goes. I think this line of reasoning is mostly based on the observations of believers in movements where the baptism is commonly pursued.

Such a large proportion of people receive tongues during Holy Spirit baptisms that it's easy to conclude that everyone ought to. But while tongues are common, I think it's a mistake to argue that they're a necessary evidence of Spirit baptisms.

For one thing, Scripture seems to say differently. As I noted, only about half of the Bible accounts of Spirit baptisms even mention tongues, and when the Bible discusses the manifestation of tongues in detail, it suggests that perhaps not everyone should expect to experience them. When Paul explained the distribution of spiritual gifts to the Corinthians, he wrote,

> To one there is given through the Spirit a message of wisdom, to another a message of knowledge by means of the same Spirit, to another faith by the same Spirit, to another gifts of healing by that one Spirit, to another miraculous powers, to another prophecy, to another distinguishing between spirits, to another speaking in different kinds of tongues, and to still another the interpretation of tongues. . . . [The Spirit] distributes them to each one, just as he determines. (1 Corinthians 12:8-11)

He later asks, "Do all have gifts of healing? Do all speak in tongues?" (1 Corinthians 12:30). Clearly, his answer is no. We all get different and particular gifts in God's plan, and no single gift is universal, which includes the gift of tongues.

Some respond to this by making a distinction between the gift of tongues and the mere exercise of speaking in tongues. Everyone should be able to speak in tongues, they say, even if only a relative few will really be gifted in it—perhaps having a proficiency that allows their tongues to be interpreted supernaturally for purposes of revelation

> We all get different and particular gifts in God's plan, and no single gift is universal.

(a practice Paul mentions in 1 Corinthians 14). Others argue that while not everyone will receive a permanent gift of tongues, everyone should experience at least a temporary manifestation of tongues during a Holy Spirit baptism.

It's probably true that some people are more gifted in supernatural tongues than others, and I think it's true that some people only receive tongues temporarily (this isn't discussed in Scripture, but I've witnessed it a number of times). But that's still no reason to think that tongues must always accompany the baptism of the Holy Spirit. It's not as if God's presence and power consists in tongues; rather, tongues are just a product of his empowerment. If a dousing of God's power manifests in a way other than tongues (say, through sudden prophesying, unnatural boldness or some overwhelming physical symptom), could anyone possibly say that the Lord's presence did not come upon the person? Of course not. God's power is one thing, and its evidences are another.

Nevertheless, it's extremely common for people to receive tongues when doused with the Spirit, and tongues seem to be unique among spiritual gifts in that they almost always initiate during a dousing— which helps explain why people readily take them as a sign of the baptism of the Spirit. Once received, the ability is almost always permanent, and it serves as a beautiful and enduringly mysterious way for us to pray with our spirit rather than our minds (1 Corinthians 14:2, 14-15).[17] It's a powerful personal tool for spiritual strengthening, so it's little wonder the Spirit chooses to make it so widespread.

How Can We Know for Sure We've Been Filled?

I think part of the reason people are so fixated on the evidence of tongues is because they're groping for assurance. They want some way to know for sure that the Spirit has filled them with his presence and power—presumably because it makes them feel more confident or beloved. The nice thing about tongues—and perhaps the reason they're so frequently used by God as an evidence of the baptism—is that they're immediate, obvious and peculiar. They quickly suggest that something significant has happened. On the other hand, I've seen some people experience tongues or other impressive manifestations only to ask afterward, "So, did it happen?" Insecurity is a stubborn thing, and in this case it's a misguided motive. The truth is, we shouldn't worry too much about whether we've received the dousing of the Spirit; we should simply focus on getting more of it.

The baptism of the Spirit is not a rite of qualification, and it doesn't determine our supernatural power status for all time. It's just a big boost. If we treat it as a status qualifier, then we run the risk of neglecting future opportunities for similar boosts.

We can always get more filling of God's presence and power, even if we've already had a Spirit-dousing experience. In Acts 4 the church's leaders are gathered together with Peter and John, celebrating the duo's release from the Sanhedrin's detention. They prayed together, "Now, Lord, consider their threats and enable your servants to speak your word with great boldness. Stretch out your hand to heal and perform signs and wonders through the name of your holy servant Jesus." Immediately, the building shook, "and they were all filled with the Holy Spirit and spoke the word of God boldly" (Acts 4:29-31). At least a portion of the people there, including Peter and John, had been previously doused in the Spirit, but now they were refilled. They got another dousing, another boost, when the presence and power of the Spirit manifested anew.

This makes sense, doesn't it? The friction of life often depletes our faith and boldness, and our desire for signs and wonders will frequently outstrip our experience to date. So, naturally, we'll benefit from more boosting, more power, more of God's manifest presence as we go. There will be a first time we experience the dousing of the Spirit's manifest presence, but there should be subsequent times as well.

So determining whether a given experience qualifies as a "baptism" is less important than continuing to experience the Spirit's dousing. Hopefully, this takes some of the tension out of the concept for worried seekers. When we talk of getting *the* dousing of the Spirit, it causes us to think about proving the experience—about necessary evidences. When we talk about *a* dousing of the Spirit, we simply think about having an empowering experience of God's manifest presence, which is much more to the point.

Early Christian leaders, for their part, seemed to be pretty flexible in the way they thought about the experience, right down to the terms they used. Sometimes the experience is described as a baptism (Acts 1:5; 11:15-17); in other places it's described as being filled (Acts 2:4; 4:31); in some places it's described as an outpouring of the Spirit (Acts 10:45); and in at least one place it's simply described as receiving the Holy Spirit (Acts 19:2). All these terms related to experiences in which the Spirit manifested observably—fire appeared, the building shook, or people broke out in tongues or prophesied or otherwise demonstrated effect. It's clear that the early believers were simply describing their experiences rather than worrying about whether their experiences fit a given term or notion. The point was to discover the experiences, not to delimit them.

If somebody says to me, "I'm not sure if I've received the baptism of the Holy Spirit yet," I respond, "Well, would you benefit from an even greater manifestation of the Spirit's presence and power in your life and ministry?" The answer should always be yes, so that helps me avoid a lot of needless discussion and lets me skip right to the part where we simply ask God for more of his manifest presence and power.

Who Gets the Baptism of the Holy Spirit?

Since the baptism of the Spirit is really just a potent experience of

God's presence, and since it's so generally empowering, every single believer should experience it. This is unquestionably how the early church thought about it.

The Spirit fell on every disciple present at the Pentecost meeting in Acts 2. And when Peter subsequently preached to onlookers, he told them, "Repent and be baptized, every one of you, in the name of Jesus Christ for the forgiveness of your sins. And you will receive the gift of the Holy Spirit. The promise is for you and your children and for all who are far off—for all whom the Lord our God will call" (Acts 2:38-39). In Peter's mind it all went together as a piece: a person chooses Jesus and then the person is filled with God's Spirit and power. One and then the other.

Jesus said that the baptism of the Spirit would bring power for the kingdom mission, and since every believer is part of the mission, it stands to reason that every believer should have the empowering experience of the baptism. So, in Acts 8, when Peter and John arrive in Samaria to meet the large number of new converts and discover that "the Holy Spirit had not yet come on any of them," they moved quickly to rectify it: "Then Peter and John placed their hands on them, and they received the Holy Spirit" (Acts 8:14-17). In Acts 19, when Paul meets some new believers in Ephesus, the first question he asks them is whether they had yet received the baptism of the Holy Spirit. He saw to it that they all received the baptism of the Spirit by the end of the day (Acts 19:1-7).

But in the Bible accounts it's also clear that the baptism is typically not something that believers receive automatically from God. In fact, it's most often something other believers have to administer to them. Everybody should experience it, but it's an experience that typically must be sought.

Some Christian theologians disagree with this, arguing instead that the biblical phrase *baptism of the Spirit* doesn't refer to a distinct manifestation of the Spirit but simply refers to the generic work of the Spirit in every believer.[18] Since we can assume the Spirit is active in the life of every believer in some way, they conclude that every believer is "baptized in the Spirit" automatically upon conversion. Accordingly, they argue, once a person has come to faith, there's nothing left to seek in terms of God's empowering presence.

This line of reasoning has some problems.

First, it doesn't explain why Jesus and the early believers felt the need to come up with the special notion of the "baptism of the Spirit." Jesus, Peter, Paul and others seem to talk about it as if it were a very specific sort of event. They speak of the works of the Spirit, but also of the "baptism of the Spirit" as if they have something quite distinct in mind.

Second, even when the Spirit had clearly been active in people, early church leaders still made a point to administer the Spirit's baptism to them as if it were an additional thing. For example, the Spirit's presence and power were abundantly evident in Philip's outreach in Samaria: there were many healings and deliverances, and as a result a large proportion of Samaritans came to faith. Nevertheless, when Peter and John showed up later, they still laid hands on the Samaritans that they might receive the baptism—"because the Holy Spirit had not yet come on any of them" (Acts 8:15-17). The Spirit had been extremely active and many had been saved, but the baptism of the Spirit had yet to occur.

Third, in every single biblical account of people getting baptized in the Spirit, the baptism takes place at a time separate from their conversion to faith, which again suggests that it is a separate and additional experience. In Acts 2 the veteran disciples received the baptism only after much prayer and waiting. In Acts 8 the Samaritans had come to faith under Philip's ministry but didn't receive the baptism of the Spirit until Peter and John showed up later. (Philip may have chosen to not administer the baptism himself because he wasn't sure if he was supposed to administer it to non-Jews.) In Acts 19, when Paul found the Ephesian believers, he made a point to ask them if they had received the baptism: he obviously assumed a person could believe without being doused in the Spirit. Later, he "placed his hands on them" and they all received the Spirit.

In my favorite biblical account of a Holy Spirit baptism, the Spirit doused people even before they had acknowledged Jesus as Lord! In Acts 10 the Lord led Peter to preach in the house of a Gentile named Cornelius. "While Peter was still speaking"—that is, before Peter had even finished explaining Jesus and the gospel—"the Holy Spirit came on all who heard the message" and they started "speaking in tongues and praising God" (Acts 10:44-46). God perhaps did it this way because Peter doubted that Gentiles should even be accepted as converts, but having seen the dousing, Peter concluded, "Surely no one can stand in the way of their being baptized with water. They have received the Holy Spirit just as we have" (Acts 10:47).

It's also possible that nonbelievers could be doused by the Spirit as a way to encourage them to accept Christ as Lord. At a recent Holy Spirit retreat, a young man from our church prayed for a nonbeliever who happened to come to "check things out." She was filled with power and spoke in tongues, and then prayed to receive Christ the following day. We've seen this sort of thing a number of times. It may be what Paul was talking about when he told the Corinthians that "tongues . . . are a sign, not for believers but for unbelievers" (1 Corinthians 14:22).

Obviously, the Spirit is free to do what he wants, when he wants, and it's certainly possible for the Spirit to baptize a new believer at the first moment of faith. But usually the ministry of the baptism of the Spirit is necessary. That is, God usually doesn't send the dousing automatically, so we have to administer it to one another. Every believer should get the baptism of the Spirit because every believer stands to benefit from it, but we need to understand that most believers will have to seek it or at least willingly accept it when offered.

You might wonder, *Why does God do it this way?* Why doesn't God just automatically douse every new believer in the power and presence of the Spirit? What's the point of God making the baptism of the Spirit its own special, distinct deal?

Part of the explanation may relate to the way God wants us to partner with him in ministry. We've talked about this at length in previous chapters. God provides power for ministry, but he expects us to make an effort to grow in that power and to apply it in the world. If he wants us to be intentional about power for ministry, it makes sense that we would have to be intentional about receiving the dousing of supernatural ministry power that comes through the Spirit's baptism. God wants us to want to receive it. When we make the intentional choice to receive the baptism of the Spirit, we are, to some extent, making an intentional choice for ministry. And that's a healthy thing.

> When we make the intentional choice to receive
> the baptism of the Spirit, we are, to some extent,
> making an intentional choice for ministry.

Even more basically, I suspect the Lord makes the choice for the Spirit's baptism distinct from our choice for Jesus because it elicits something distinct in our hearts. It's one thing to say, "I believe in Jesus," and a somewhat different thing to say, "I want the manifest presence of God overflowing in me." Obviously, we follow Jesus because we want God in our lives, but the dousing of the Spirit is such a profound and immediate intimacy that it merits its own decision.

A person who is doused in the presence of the Spirit, who feels the power of that presence, can have no illusions about a distant God and no illusions about a "safe" or controllable God either. It's good for believers to take a moment to consider that. I have known many long-time believers to grow very sober the first time they observe someone getting baptized in the Spirit. "Wow," one said to me, "that somehow seems a little less, uh, measured than what I'm used to." And he was right. Insofar as we have to make a distinct choice to pursue or receive that degree of intimacy, we'll have to consider the boundaries, or the happy lack of boundaries, we've erected in our walk with God. That too strikes me as a healthy thing.

How Do We Go About Getting the Baptism of the Spirit?

Finally, we get to the good part: How do we go about getting the baptism of the Spirit, and how do we administer it to others who want it? Having discussed some of the stickier issues, I'd expect this part to seem pretty simple.

Here's a basic ministry model for the baptism of the Spirit: a believer who has been baptized with the Spirit lays hands on a believer who wants a dousing and asks God to let his Spirit flow. The believer who is receiving the baptism should be encouraged to receive. And that's pretty much it.

As the Scriptures make clear, the Spirit can fall on anyone he chooses, but as with other sorts of supernatural ministry, the manifestation of the Spirit's dousing typically flows from person to person, which is why we lay on hands or do similar things. In Acts 9 Jesus appears to Saul in a powerful supernatural visitation on the road to Damascus, manifesting strongly before Saul, speaking audibly to him and even striking him with temporary blindness. But in spite of the heavy supernatural quality of this experience, the Lord still opts to send Ananias a few days later to lay hands on Saul that he might be filled with the Spirit. The Lord loves to partner with human ministers when he can.

When we administer the baptism of the Spirit to someone, we're not introducing the person to the general presence of God (as if it were a conversion experience); we're imparting to him or her a particular manifestation of God's presence and power. To *impart* means to share something that we have. Accordingly, it's helpful if those who are administering the baptism are themselves doused in God's manifest presence and power. So before we do impartation times at my church, I encourage my ministry teams to get "as soaked as possible"— to seek a fresh filling of the Spirit for themselves. I've found that things that increase the flow of God's power in us generally—authority, faith, consecration—also make the impartation of God's power flow well through us, which isn't surprising. The bottom line: to be a good minister of the baptism of the Spirit, it helps to be prepared.

Those basic guidelines aside, I'd have to say that the only real rule about the ministry of the baptism is that there are no hard and fast rules. In Acts 10, as I mentioned, the Spirit doused a house full of Gentiles who hadn't even acknowledged Jesus as Lord yet. It's hard to put the Spirit in a box.

One of my first experiences in administering the baptism was actually over the phone. Shortly after I was first doused in the Spirit, I called a friend back home and told her about it. I prayed for her briefly, asking God to send her a similar gift at some point, and after we hung up, she suddenly started praying in tongues.

Similarly, a young woman at my church got her first dousing after praying over the phone with a friend during a lull in her work day. The Spirit fell upon her and she broke out in tongues for the first time while sitting at the reception desk in her office space.

On numerous occasions, dubious observers have come to our impartation services, standing carefully on the periphery to watch, only to find themselves suddenly overwhelmed with the Spirit's presence and empowered with breakout manifestations of spiritual gifts. Such experiences are not really out of the blue—the people were observing an impartation service, after all—but they're not formulaic either. I think they happen just because the Spirit is manifestly present, and because he has an extraordinarily outgoing personality. Jesus said that the Father is more eager to give us the Holy Spirit than an earthly father is eager to feed his kids (Luke 11:11-13), and it often shows.

Of course, despite the Lord's inherent eagerness, you'll experience ministry times in which nothing seems to happen for the person to whom you're ministering. Since the ministry of the baptism involves human partnership with God, human stuff can get in the way and otherwise shape the experience. We know that stuff like fear, lack of faith or issues of obedience or consecration can influence the flow of God's power through us or into us. None of these things are really showstoppers, and they won't necessarily prevent the Spirit from dousing people sovereignly if he chooses, but insofar as the baptism comes as a result of human ministry, it's possible that our humanity will make the process more difficult. The question is, how should we handle it?

The first step is to guard against jumping to silly conclusions. It would be very wrong to assume that a person who doesn't immediately experience a powerful manifestation of the Spirit's presence is somehow rejected by God or destined for a dull life. God's desire to douse a person must be understood separately from the process of dousing the person. Just as Jesus had to twice lay hands on the blind man of Bethsaida to cure him (Mark 8:22-26), you might need to minister repeatedly to people before they receive an impartation of the Spirit's filling. If the process takes a while, that's OK.

That brings up the second step: keep at it. It's helpful to remember

that the baptism of the Spirit is not some sort of one-time qualification event. A person who's doused once with the Spirit should
seek more dousing later. So, whether a person is overcome with
powerful sensations and speaks in tongues or feels absolutely
nothing, I encourage the person to continue to pursue the Spirit's
filling. Rather than hearing a person say, "Nothing happened," I
would prefer him or her to say, "I want more!"

I suspect it's sometimes actually helpful to people if the manifestation of the Spirit's filling doesn't happen immediately. After Jesus
gave his final instructions to the disciples regarding the baptism of the
Spirit, they still had to persevere in prayer for ten days before the Spirit
came in power. The Lord let Saul sit for three days in prayer and fasting
before sending Ananias to heal his eyes and fill him with the Spirit.
Why such delays? I'm not sure, but I think it occasionally helps us to
stretch for more of God or to spend time concentrating our desires.

Finally, as with all other supernatural ministries, when you administer the baptism of the Spirit, you'll want to stay sensitive to
people's reactions in order to shepherd them as needed. People
sometimes have strong emotional reactions when the Spirit comes.
Most often these are joyful, but occasionally they're negative because some folks—whether they're aware of it or not—are afraid of
or angry with God, and when his Spirit comes, these people can
freak out a bit. Such reactions are ultimately helpful because they
reveal deep-seated burdens and give people an opportunity to deal
with God in his clear presence—sort of a face-to-face conversation.

Dealing with people's emotional wounds can be intricate business,
but I typically encourage these people to receive whatever they can
from the Spirit during impartation ministry. I'll say, "The Lord's
presence is here, so why don't you just stand peacefully with him and
see if he brings you anything that feels helpful?" The Holy Spirit is
the Spirit of adoption, and I know that if people give him a chance, a

taste of his presence often accomplishes more in them than any amount of clever counseling would. As one relieved brother recently exclaimed after his first encounter with the Spirit's dousing, "He's here for me! He's here for me!"

You'll also find that the ministry of Holy Spirit baptism occasionally flushes out demons, and you should be ready for it. When the Spirit's presence begins to manifest strongly, demons will sometimes manifest strongly in the people they've afflicted, because demons get very uneasy in the presence of God. Again, such reactions are not a bad thing, because they reveal the need for a little deliverance ministry. We're always happy to do deliverance ministry because it leads to freedom. At our most recent Holy Spirit retreat, as soon as I offered my opening prayer of impartation over the crowd, a young man standing behind me collapsed in a heap and started vomiting. A few young ministers calmly walked over to him and completed the deliverance, and a few minutes later the man was dancing and hugging anyone within reach—all before we'd even started laying hands on people. The manifest presence of God stirs stuff up, and if we're prepared and willing, it's all helpful.

In sum, the process of the Spirit's baptism is a pretty simple one. Most often, one believer passes the Spirit's dousing to another. Ministers will do well to be prepared. Sometimes the process will require a little perseverance, and occasionally ministers will have to deal sensitively with dramatic reactions people have when the Spirit comes powerfully.

One of the things I enjoy most about the ministry of the Spirit's baptism is that it's always fresh. The manifestation of the Spirit's presence is a fundamental kingdom experience, but the Lord has such a personal way with people that it seems new every time. It's theologically profound and supernaturally intense, but it's also just a lot of fun.

Fruitfulness

Jesus said that a "tree is known by its fruit" (Matthew 12:33 ESV), and my parting shot in our discussion of the baptism of the Spirit is that we should always remember this. The point of being filled with the manifest power and presence of the Spirit is to become more fruitful. Part of the operation of the Spirit in our lives will be the personal fruit it creates in us: Paul underscores "love, joy, peace, patience, kindness, goodness, faithfulness, gentleness and self-control" as proper "fruit of the Spirit" (Galatians 5:22-23). But Jesus assured his disciples that the baptism of the Spirit would also give them "power to be witnesses" to the ends of the earth. As soon as you receive a dousing of the Spirit, one of your main goals should be to give it away, again and again. As soon as you're "clothed with power from on high," you should try to minister in power to the world. The baptism of the Spirit is a gift the Father gives to you, but he does not give it just for you. It's supposed to be shared.

> The point of being filled with the manifest
> power and presence of the Spirit is
> to become more fruitful.

Every believer has others to shape and influence—people who are downstream in the kingdom flow. Maybe you don't feel a particular need for "power from on high," but chances are somebody in your stream will need it desperately. Maybe you don't feel a particular need for any sort of supernatural ministry or experience, but somebody downstream of you will. And you only get to pass on what you have.

Interaction

I admit that I've always been a little messed up, but at least some of it has been circumstantial—I think.

My parents split immediately after my birth, and for complicated reasons my dad, grandma and I spent my formative years running around the country, hiding from the cops, living under aliases. When I eventually started school, I actually didn't know what my real name was. I attended seven schools in eight years, lived with different family members at different times and finally settled with my dad and new stepfamily in a beautiful but economically depressed mill town in Oregon. We waded through the typical drug and alcohol stuff. Two out of three of us kids managed to graduate high school, and the third eventually got an equivalency certificate. In all, everybody did pretty well.

But somewhere in the displacements of childhood, I started experiencing episodes of intense depression. Beginning around age five or six I became haunted with the idea of suicide, which, I'm told, is not a sign of healthy childhood development. I had little ways of generating emotional discipline when I needed it. For instance, I would occasionally just stop eating for a while (a week and a half at most), and sometimes I would go for days without speaking unless I was forced.

I also put God on contract. I made a deal with him: I would faithfully shrug off the challenges of my early years in exchange for God giving me a uniquely awesome life later on. Mind you, I never actually got God's approval on this deal, but I relied on it emotionally, and in some ways it served its purpose and even seemed to bear out for a while. I managed to hit all the right notes in my teens, got a ticket to Stanford University, won a bunch of academic awards, picked up a fine wife, got a scholarship for grad school, strolled through my Ph.D. coursework and started publishing in national academic journals.

And then the depression came back—with a vengeance, for a long time.

I'm sure its return was partly the result of my old handicaps resurfacing, but I also think it was complicated by an extended season of intense disappointments.

For instance, though I did well in grad school and won a fairly prestigious postdoctoral fellowship to Harvard, when I started looking for a job as a professor, no one would hire me. In fact, in four years on the market, not a single university was interested enough in my work to give me a job interview. After sinking nine years into grad school and research, I was crushed.

Some health challenges added to my stress. For almost two years I suffered with abdominal pain that no one could diagnose until they finally stuck a camera in me and found a nasty little growth.

Happily, during that time Sonya and I got pregnant. It was a tremendous blessing to our marriage, which had chafed under my depression. But then we lost the baby to miscarriage. Later that year we got pregnant again, but we lost that child too. A bit later we had another miscarriage, and then another, and another. By the end, we had lost seven babies. The doctors had no idea why.

Right after our first miscarriage, my great-grandmother, to whom I was extremely close, passed away.

After our second, my aunt passed away, and after the third, my dog died.

I had quit my academic career in discouragement and humiliation, and took a job at a startup software company. I played a significant role in developing the company, often working ninety-hour weeks. Twice I went for months without pay until the company solidified. Then I was suddenly fired under very questionable pretenses. Sonya and I were expecting at the time. The company owed me a fair bit of money, but I had no good way to claim it.

Ministry offered some refuge. After helping plant a church in Chicago, Sonya and I had hooked up with a church plant near Harvard. She took a job on the ministry staff, and we both served there fruitfully for a few years. But I managed to offend a couple of the pastors, though not by anything I actually said or did, which made reconciliation hard. They suspected that I secretly disapproved of them and their work. I suggested they might be misreading the strain I was showing in life (and I was definitely showing strain), but my denials were taken as being uncooperative, and the whole silly thing just got so weird that Sonya and I were forced to leave the church community to ensure peace. Of all the disappointments in that period, Sonya has always claimed this one was the most painful. We were working so diligently and dealing with so very much that it seemed absurd to lose our church as well. It also meant that Sonya lost her paycheck, and since I didn't have one either, we were pretty broke. Some friends let us live in their basement.

Professional losses, physical pain, deaths, miscarriages, broken relationships, financial wipeout and, of course, depression. I was punch-drunk. During my frequent sleepless nights, I couldn't even speak to God. All I could do was inhale, and then exhale, and then resolve to inhale again. I didn't pray; I just breathed unto God. Like Jonah, I sometimes told God that I was "angry enough to die." Why couldn't he give me a break? What on earth was he thinking? Maybe I did want to die.

Then one day as I drank coffee and thought about death (I was loads of fun at parties), I remembered Jesus' teaching: "Whoever wants to save their life will lose it, but whoever loses their life for me will save it" (Luke 9:24). I remembered that Paul told believers to "count as lost" all desires apart from kingdom ones. That started me on a lengthy consideration of what it meant to live as a dead man— as a man who had nothing left to lose, who couldn't be thrown off by disappointment and who simply surrendered his existence to God.

I read up on traditions of self-mortification and went on lengthy food fasts, kept all-night prayer vigils and did hidden service exercises to whittle down the flesh. I resolved to go for periods without ever speaking about myself, and for months I forbade myself to complain about anything, ever. I tried whatever I could think of to get free from self-regard. It was emotional management, but it was also spiritual discipline, and this time I didn't try to make any deals with God.

It's a dicey proposition when a very depressed person launches on a campaign of intense self-denial, but in the end it started paying off. I went from gasping despondency to simple mourning, from hurricane anger to a sort of dignified disappointment.

And it was in that condition that I traveled to Colorado with a few friends to attend a conference on supernatural ministry.

On the second to last day, a famous supernatural minister spoke, and I decided to ask him to pray for me when he was done, to help me in my healing process. But as I walked toward the front of the conference hall, an acquaintance stopped me to ask for my prayers.

By the time I was through with her, the famous fellow had left the building. Undaunted, I approached a member of the guy's ministry team and asked if she would pray for me instead. "Sure," she said, and laid a hand on my shoulder, but then she apparently got distracted and without a word walked away, leaving me standing there like a frustrated panhandler.

I got upset.

I stalked over to the one remaining member of the ministry team I could find and said, "Look, I've been depressed. Pray for me!" Her name tag identified her as Bobbie from Oklahoma. She prayed for me for a few moments and then launched into bold and fluent prophesying. But her "revelations" about my circumstances were glaringly inaccurate. I mean, not even close. A big zero. And just as I opened my mouth to thank her and excuse myself politely, the Spirit fell upon me and I dropped to my knees as if I'd been struck. For the only time in my life, I had an out-of-body experience.

I could vaguely hear the rumbling sounds of the conference hall, but they sounded miles away. I seemed to be in a little room, almost completely dark. And then I felt the presence of the Father enter. Without spoken words, he said two things to me: "Good job. I love you." And then he withdrew. That's all there was to it.

When I "came back" some time later, I was still kneeling on the floor. Bobbie stayed with me for a few minutes, and then a couple friends came to sit with me while I sobbed on the carpet. When it was time to close the building, my friends lifted me up, carried me out to the parking lot and rolled me into the back of an SUV. Still, I blubbered. I would end up weeping through most of the night. And though my life circumstances actually got even more difficult over the next several months, and though the ten years since have been filled with challenges and mistakes of every sort, that day would mark the end of my depression, once and for all.

The lasting point of any supernatural event—any healing, deliverance, prophetic revelation, empowerment—is defined by the degree to which it provides or encourages a direct encounter with the living God. Supernatural experiences can be materially restorative, and they can provide testimonies for skeptics and signs to believers, but most fundamentally they're just interactions with God. And bless me if I haven't sorely needed them.

I have lots of provocative stories about supernatural ministry, but the supernatural experiences that have shaped me most are the simple, intimate ones—the personal interactions in which I've gotten to feel, for a short while, the manifest presence of God there for me. And for all of us who try so hard to be supernatural people, learning as we go—who shrug off the world and embrace the weirdness of the kingdom, who show up where we shouldn't and try the impossible, who sacrifice big chunks of ourselves and relish God's glory in the grit—for us, in the end, the one supernatural encounter we want most is the one in which God shows up and says, "Good job. I love you." Just thinking about it could make you cry.

The day after my tearful encounter with the Lord, I got a little good-natured teasing from my friend Chelsea. "Gee, Jordan, I don't think I've ever seen you gush before. I'm surprised you could do it without hurting yourself!"

In my defense, I'm not sure anyone could justifiably call it gushing. Sure, I wept for hours, but it's not like I talked on and on about it. In fact, I can only remember repeating one thing: "I'm so thankful I'm his son. I'm so thankful I'm his son."

Appendix

Tips for Pastors

I recently went to a doctor because I had some persistent stomach pain.

"What do you do for a living?" he asked.

"I'm the head pastor at a church in town," I said.

"Oh, then you have an ulcer."

"Um, why do you say that?"

"Because every single pastor who's come into my office has an ulcer," he said.

"Seriously?"

"Yeah. The stress. You guys take your work home. Your schedules are crazy. Everybody's coming to you with impossible problems. I deal with bodies," he noted. "You have to deal with everything."

"Good point," I said.

"Plus, everybody's always judging you, right? You're Mr. Spiritual, so everything you do is up for inspection—what you say, how you spend time, what you buy."

"Well, sometimes."

"And *churches*! Everybody has expectations of how things should go. You want to be everybody's friend, but you're also in charge."

"Sure," I said.

"Plus, when regular families rest together on the weekends or celebrate on holidays, that's when you get extra busy. I can imagine what that means for managing a marriage and kids."

"OK, I get it."

"And it's not like you get paid well."

"So, when's the part where you make me feel better?"

It turned out I didn't have an ulcer, but he almost gave me one.

Being a pastor is hard. Bringing supernatural ministry to a church is particularly challenging. Perhaps you're a pastor who's thinking about bringing supernatural ministry to the church you lead. Supernatural ministry is hard. Leading people through change is hard. Put them together and it's sometimes exponentially hard.

But the local church pastor is uniquely equipped to inspire and train large numbers of believers to move forward in supernatural ministries—something I'd dearly love to see. If you follow these tips well, things will still be challenging. That's just how it is. But supernatural ministry can change lives, and that's what pastors care about most.

1. If you're going to lead a congregation into supernatural ministries, you can't lead from behind. You might be tempted to encourage others to forge ahead in supernatural ministry while you stand slightly apart, cheering successes but remaining insulated from mistakes and messiness. This is the "Independent Manager" model. It does not serve well. If you don't participate aggressively in supernatural ministries, then people will see supernatural ministry as an exception rather than the model to follow. You don't help your people by maintaining distance.

So make sure you lay hands on a sick person in front of everyone. Give or receive prophecies in public. Demonstrate supernatural ministry to your congregation, clumsy as it may sometimes seem. Beyond the leadership these acts provide, you'll be showing your supernatural pioneers that you're sharing their sacrifices. That will encourage them in the necessary sacrifices of supernatural ministries.

2. Make sure everyone understands that the key to doing supernatural ministry is to do things that develop God's power in us. Stress this point early and often. People tend to think that God simply does miracles or he doesn't, or that a minister is gifted or not. If they understand that supernatural ministry is about growing in power, they will see the potential for growth in themselves and others.

3. Use small groups and limited venues in the beginning to practice supernatural ministries, train novices and generate testimonies. Once you've gathered some good stories, feature supernatural ministry in more public meetings. Good testimonies are the key to going public because they spread faith and inspire others to join in. Ultimately, you want to cultivate broad participation throughout your congregation because you leverage everyone's spiritual gifts that way, and because broad ownership will improve the positive faith environment in your church. Plus, as I mentioned in chapter four, you want your church to be known publicly for supernatural ministry in order to attract those who need it. Make supernatural ministries part of your Sunday morning line-up or convene public healing services or otherwise open things up.

4. Avoid telling secondhand testimonies. Don't let people share about a guy they heard about. If you're going to share testimonies, make sure they're about your community or people directly connected to you. There are two reasons for this. First, hearsay is less trustworthy as evidence, so it tends to invite criticism. Second, secondhand stories invoke the question "Why doesn't that happen here?" You're trying to convince people not simply that God does supernatural things but that God will do supernatural things through them.

5. As I've suggested throughout the book, be open about mistakes

and failures in supernatural ministry. A failure can be helpful if, in being honest about it, you demonstrate authenticity to your people. Authentic people are trustworthy, and people are often concerned about trustworthiness in supernatural ministry. Everybody will know that things aren't working perfectly. So when you're open about it—and confident in spite of it—they'll be reassured that it's being dealt with sensibly and graciously. You'll demonstrate that failure and mistakes are simply part of the growth process.

6. Finally, go out of your way to create a culture that honors risks. You do this when you try risky things yourself and when you celebrate the risky things that other people try—even if those things don't work out perfectly. At my church, we give an annual award for "Most Spectacular Whiff" to an individual who failed at some spiritual venture that was nonetheless worth trying. We also make a point to share stories from members who are in the midst of trying risky things. Everyone roots for them, come what may.

You should already have a risk-honoring culture at your church, because faith doesn't grow without risk. But since supernatural ministries often require growth in faith, you'll probably want to make a special point to honor risk when you can. Happily, supernatural ministries provide lots of opportunities to risk!

If you're a pastor of a local church, your job is to build a powerful kingdom community. It's a tall order that requires your people to have transformative experiences. Supernatural ministries are a great tool for providing such experiences to both seekers who receive the ministry and believers who practice it. Supernatural ministries are otherworldly by definition, and you want your church to be an otherworldly place for everyone who enters. You want it to show otherworldly love, otherworldly generosity, otherworldly fearlessness and, yes, otherworldly power. Supernatural ministries are an excellent way to get people to shake off the bonds of the normal world.

Questions for Review
and Group Discussion

The following questions are designed to encourage review and discussion of the material in *Miracle Work*. The questions follow the order in which topics are presented in the book.

Supernatural Ministry and Power

1. Successful supernatural ministries help us care for other people, but they also aid our own life and faith walk. What does it mean to be a supernatural, otherworldly person? How do supernatural ministries help us get there?

2. God has chosen to partner with us to get things done in the world. Why? Why does ministry require so much work and sacrifice from us?

3. What is the biggest key to becoming more effective in supernatural ministries such as healing, deliverance and prophecy?

4. Describe the four important elements we should think about when trying to increase the flow of God's supernatural power in us. How do we grow in each?

The Ministry of Healing

1. Describe the process of engaging in healing ministry.

2. What are some ways we might increase our supernatural power

when we're trying to heal someone?

3. How can we help people navigate the intense emotions that often surround sickness and healing? What understandings might we share with people who are wary of disappointment?

The Ministry of Deliverance

1. Generally, how do demons gain control over people?

2. In what ways might we be able to discern if a person is afflicted by a demon?

3. How do we make a demon leave?

4. How do we tell if a demon has left?

The Ministry of Prophecy

1. What are some of the different ways in which God might speak to us directly?

2. How can we tell if it's really God speaking to us? How do we get better at this discernment?

3. How can we get better at understanding the prophetic messages we receive?

4. What should we keep in mind when delivering prophecies to others?

The Ministry of Intercession

1. What's the difference between simple prayers of petition and the full ministry of intercession?

2. In general, what do we need to accomplish to forge an intercessory bond with people? What sort of things might we do to accomplish it?

The Baptism of the Holy Spirit

1. What is the baptism of the Holy Spirit? What is it for?

2. What should we do if we want to receive the filling of the Spirit?

3. How do we administer the filling of the Holy Spirit to others?

Notes

[1] Irenaeus, *Against Heresies*, bk. 2, chap. 32, section 4, trans. Alexander Roberts and William Rambaut, in *Ante-Nicene Fathers*, vol. 1, ed. Alexander Roberts, James Donaldson and A. Cleveland Coxe (Buffalo, NY: Christian Literature Publishing Co., 1885). This translation is widely available online.

[2] Origen, *Against Celsus*, bk. 1, chap. 46, trans. Frederick Crombie, in *Ante-Nicene Fathers*, vol. 4, ed. Alexander Roberts, James Donaldson and A. Cleveland Coxe (Buffalo, NY: Christian Literature Publishing Co., 1885). This translation is widely available online.

[3] Indeed, Athanasius is probably most famous today for his globally revered *Life of Anthony*, which might just be the most popular biography in Christian history.

[4] Augustine, *The City of God*, bk. 22, chap. 8, trans. Marcus Dods. In *Nicene and Post-Nicene Fathers*, First Series, vol. 2, ed. Philip Schaff (Buffalo, NY: Christian Literature Publishing Co., 1887). This translation is widely available online.

[5] We have two documents written by Patrick, the more illuminating being his *Confessions*, which details numerous accounts of miracle working in his battle against the Druids for the heart of Ireland. The miracles, prophecies and angelic visions of Columba were chronicled by his successor, Adomnan of Iona, in his *Life of Columba*. Adomnan wrote expressly to preserve the details of the saint's supernatural feats.

[6] See Venerable Bede, *Ecclesiastical History of England*, chap. 31. Bede, quoted from the letter in his *Ecclesiastical History*, originally published in A.D. 731. Accounts of miracles color the entire history, which is considered among the most scholarly and reputable works of the age.

[7] See John Howie, *The Scots Worthies*, ed. W. H. Carslaw (1775; reprint, Edinburgh: Oliphant, Anderson & Ferrier, 1902), pp. 27-38, 60-63, 120-33. See also Jack Deere, *Surprised by the Voice of God* (Grand Rapids: Zondervan, 1998), chap. 5, for a summary discussion of prophetic works during the early Scottish Reform era and the historical scholarship that recorded it.

[8] See Robert Fleming, *The Fulfillment of Scripture* (Rotterdam: n.p., 1671), pp. 416-40, as discussed in Deere, *Surprised by the Voice of God*, chap. 5.

[9]*The Journal of John Wesley*, entry of April 17, 1739, in *The Journal of the Rev. John Wesley*, vol. 2, ed. Nehemiah Curnock (London: Charles H. Kelly, 1827). This version is widely available online.

[10]Ibid., entry of August 15, 1750.

[11]For Wesley, see his *Journals* from October 14, 1735, to November 29, 1745, in *The Works of John Wesley*, 3rd ed., (Grand Rapids: Baker, 1991), vol. 1. For Edwards, see especially "The Distinguishing Marks of a Work of the Spirit of God," in various publications and anthologies. See also "An Account of the Revival of Religion on North Hampton in 1740-42, Communicated in a Letter to a Minister in Boston," in *Jonathan Edwards on Revival* (Carlisle, UK: Banner of Truth Trust, 1984).

[12]See "The Narrative of Sarah Edwards," in Sereno Dwight, *The Works of President Edwards: With a Memoir of His Life* (New York: Carvill, 1830), 1:14.

[13]There is a more detailed discussion of deliverance ministry in chapter five.

[14]There is a more detailed discussion about discerning the personal, prophetic direction of the Lord in chapter six.

[15]We'll talk more about impartation in the upcoming chapter on the filling of the Holy Spirit.

[16]Charles Finney, *Power from On High* (Fort Washington, PA: Christian Literature Crusade), p. 10.

[17]Neuroscientific laboratory research has actually shown that when people speak in tongues, the speech centers of their brains do not activate as one would expect in speech, and neither do the control centers of the brain. This suggests, as believers have always claimed, that tongue speakers are neither constructing nor precisely controlling the speech that pours from them. See for example Andrew B. Newberg et al., "Cerebral Blood Flow During the Complex Vocalization Task of Glossolalia," *Journal of Nuclear Medicine Meeting Abstracts* 47, supp. 1 (2006); Andrew B. Newberg et al., "The Measurement of Regional Cerebral Blood Flow During Glossolalia: A Preliminary SPECT Study," *Psychiatry Research: Neuroimaging* 148, no. 1 (2006): 67-71; and Timothy Arthur Jones, "Electroencephalogical Correlates of Glossolalic Christian Prayer" (master's thesis, University of Idaho, 1981).

[18]Perhaps the most respected proponent of this view is the esteemed theologian John Stott. For his full presentation on the subject, see John R. W. Stott, *Baptism and Fullness: The Work of the Holy Spirit Today* (Downers Grove, IL: InterVarsity Press, 1975).